Li WITHDRAWN nt

A g

Other books edited by Teresa Allissa Citro

Parenting the Child with Learning Disabilities:
The Experts Speak

Lifetime Management for Success: Adults with Learning Disabilities

Edited by

Teresa Allissa Citro
Executive Director
Learning Disabilities Association of Massachusetts

Learning Disabilities Association of Massachusetts

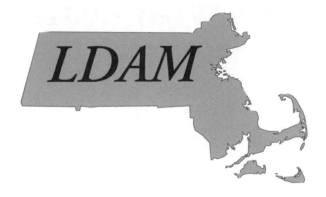

This book is dedicated to Antonio and Teresa, my parents, who have taught me to value, respect and make the best of whatever life offers. All I am and all I hope to be I owe to you. Thanks for being such loving, wonderful parents and believing the best of me.

Contents

Preface

This book looks at the issues adults with learning disabilities encounter. Adults with learning disabilities meet many challenges in life. They have to understand their learning disabilities and how these disabilities many impact relationships and work life. When adults return to school they must face the struggles associated with learning.

It is my hope that readers will be encouraged never to give up. Each person brings strengths and gifts to the world to be appreciated. If you are a professional reading this book, you can ensure that the children and adults with learning disabilities who cross your path have your understanding, encouragement and help to achieve their aspirations. Regardless of learning disabilities, everyone has the ability to reach their full potential.

Acknowledgements

The Learning Disabilities Association of Massachusetts would like to thank Anchor to Windward, Inc. of Marblehead, Massachusetts, a program that supports independent living for adults with learning disabilities and Hills Department Store Company, Canton, Massachusetts for its generous grants to fund the publication of this book. Without their support, Lifetime Management for Success: Adults with Learning Disabilities would not exist.

Many thanks go to Debra Berger and Moira Munns for their editorial assistance; thanks to Michele D'Agostino for assisting with the art design of the cover; thanks to "The Boston Parents' Paper" for the use of the photographs for the book cover; and Waltham Printing Services, Inc. for always coming to the rescue, thank you Joe Brownstein.

The Board of Directors of the Learning Disabilities Association of Massachusetts, Jane Derman-Kilgallon, President, Maureen Riley and Dr. Jerome J. Schultz vice-presidents, Ruth and Lee Glazerman, Leslie Goldberg, Michelle Pastore, Dr. Stephen Rothenberg, Robin Welch and Lorraine Zimmerman represents an assembly of individuals whose lives are both exceptional and inspirational. I have learned so much from all of you. Your dedication to children and adults with learning disabilities is admired, respected, and valued. Massachusetts is fortunate to have such a dedicated group that has and continues to make a difference in the lives of individuals with learning disabilities. Without your support and hard work there would not be an LDAM. I feel as if I have been favored to have the opportunity to work with you. I truly believe I have the best job in the world. Thank you for supporting me and for helping me to grow. As we all have worked together lives of individuals have been touched .

Finally, I thank the authors who have each contributed a chapter for this book; Dr. Loring Brinckerhoff, Dr. Noel Gregg, Peter and Patricia Latham, Nancy Paine, Maureen Riley, Dr. Stephen Rothenberg, Dr. Jerry Schultz, and Dr. Sharon Zimmerman; and to Sally Smith for her sensitive and insightful forward. As a result of your love for people, many have reached their goals in life. Thank you for giving of yourselves in such a generous manner.

Introduction

Successful Lifetime Strategies
for Adults

Sally L. Smith

Sally L. Smith is founder/director of The Lab School and a professor at American University, in Washington, D.C. She is also the author of No Easy Answers: The Learning Disabled Child at Home and at School *(Bantam 1995) and* Succeeding Against the Odds *(Tarcher 1991).*

Have you met the extraordinarily competent adult whose writing looks like chicken scratch?

Perhaps you know the bright adult, who just doesn't seem to be put together well, who looks scattered, and whose belongings appear everywhere?

Have you seen the adult who's a genius with his hands, putting together and fixing things, but cannot problem solve with words and doesn't understand jokes?

Or have you met the adult who's a disaster with her hands, can barely open her change purse, but has an incredible presence, a poise, and the correct word for every occasion?

Do you know the young woman who is basically very kind but has a penchant for saying the wrong thing at the wrong time and hurts people's feelings?

Have you met the able young man who personalizes everything, and over-reacts to many statements and situations?

Perhaps you know the talented photographer who reads so slowly and can barely spell a word?

Or you may be friends with the woman who can't remember anyone's name, address or telephone number?

Do you know the very competent CEO of a company who is known for getting lost in buildings and has a terrible time finding his car in the parking lot?

Have you met the excellent recreation worker who puts the child's left shoe on the right foot and the right on the left?

Do you know the charming sales person who has no sense of time and doesn't know if it's been a half hour or two hours since she left for lunch?

Have you seen the talented artist who cannot balance a checkbook and cannot remember to write down the amount paid out and the date?

Or does the bright college student you know speak so impressively in his classes, but doesn't hand in his papers and fails?

If you recognize yourself in these descriptions it might be that you are one of these intelligent, often gifted, adults with learning disabilities who has to work so much harder than those in the average population to succeed. I'm sure you have met a number of bright adults who are under employed adults, who have trouble reading, spelling, doing math, organizing their thoughts, and expressing themselves orally or in writing, adults who are as exceptional in their abilities as in their disabilities. Some are wonderful athletes; others are clumsy. Some are unusually artistic; others are not. Some are incredible talkers; others are silent. Many are wonderfully social; others have no friends.

These adults might have a learning disability. It's the particular constellation of difficulties, the quantity, the quality, the intensity of problems, the patterns of learning, that point to a neurologically-based problem called learning disabilities. Something is wrong with the wiring of the brain, akin to a telephone switchboard with loose wires, somehow short circuiting the incoming and outgoing messages. Learning disabilities can affect every area of a person's life and interfere with academic achievement, recreational activities, emotional and social life. They are all-pervasive. Many adults rise above their learning disabilities to pursue effectively their chosen fields of endeavor. Their learning disabilities become an inconvenience, a nuisance, that must be dealt with every day, but still allow for astonishing creativity, originality, and resourcefulness. Most people with learning disabilities are excellent problem solvers. They have to be!

Many adults who looked typical as children didn't learn typically and never received the individualized, specialized help in school they needed. They were very smart and looked too good! They tested too well, particularly on intelligence tests. Often they were tested in third or fourth grade and again in sixth grade and once or twice more in high school, but frequently they were not identified as having a learning disability. In school, they met the minimum of standards. Many of them suffered terribly in classes of algebra, chemistry, and foreign language. Almost all of them had great difficulty writing and spelling. They became lost between the cracks – barely passing, failing, repeating courses, repeating grades, feeling stupid, feeling bad about themselves, and yet getting by through their own clever machinations, and by putting in an interminable number of extra hours.

Adults with learning disabilities tend to feel bad about themselves, sometimes rotten. They feel they are no good, useless, second-class citizens. Unfortunately, they tend to believe what they have been accused of all their lives by ignorant people:

> *You're lazy.*
> *You're unmotivated.*
> *You could do it if you would just try.*

And here they are, trying their hearts out! No wonder many of them feel life is unfair! Some adults will purposely not put out efforts to succeed because they don't want to risk failure and defeat again. They would prefer to be seen as having a behavior problem rather than viewed as "dumb." They say, "I won't," rather than acknowledge "I can't." Counteracting the feeling of being stupid becomes one of the most important goals to achieve for adults with learning disabilities and for those who work with them.

The pain is deep. The humiliation is constant. Their radar is out continually to avoid situations where they might look inadequate or stupid. Adults with learning disabilities at the Night School of The Lab School of Washington tell us that since kindergarten they knew something was wrong. They say they watched their five-year-old peers pick up information, draw and construct things, learn letters and words, manipulate numbers, remember names of movies seen, repeat stories that were read to them – all things that were difficult for them. It was back in kindergarten that they started to build up their defense systems against experiencing more failure. I call these "masks," such as the mask of the class clown who can get everyone to laugh so the students don't pay attention to what he cannot do. Unfortunately, a great deal of energy goes into developing and maintaining these masks rather than releasing energy to problem solve, to find different ways to accomplish tasks and to learn effectively in school.

The raw emotions of anger and guilt frequently become too prominent a part of the lives of adults with learning disabilities. They feel the guilt of letting their parents and loved ones down. And the anger at the unfairness of it all can consume them. Sometimes, anger prevents them from developing strategies to improve their learning. Sometimes, anger turns into the positive energy of a fierce determination to succeed. Many adults with learning disabilities work ten times harder than anyone else and, because of their effort, often land on top!

The abilities of people with learning disabilities need to be unearthed. But, there are many abilities and personal strengths that these adults carry around with them and tend to downplay. Adults with learning disabilities can be very hard on themselves. They need to have friends and family and mates who keep pointing out very specifically the things they do well. They need the feedback on their successes as well as on their mistakes. How we wish employers could learn to give specific praise, so crucial to every person feeling good about himself or herself. Adults with learning disabilities need to know themselves better than other people do.

This is what I do well.
This is what I have trouble with.
These are the techniques that work best for me.

When they know themselves well, they can advocate well for themselves and they can become their own best advocates. Adults with learning disabilities must have the power to interpret their needs to others and make their lives better. They cannot remain passive. They can be agents of change and help improve the very quality of their own lives.

This book, published by the Learning Disabilities Association of Massachusetts, will help adults with learning disabilities and the people who live and work with them understand the nature of learning disabilities, how they are diagnosed, and how they impact all relationships. The book looks at special problems in the workplace, in colleges, graduate schools, and in daily living, as well as at the legal issues in education and work. Read it several times. Use it as a resource.

There is nothing more important in life than to feel comfortable in our own skins. We are who we are with all the blemishes and warts, limps and fears. What matters most is what we do with what we have. It is the quality of life lived that fuels the human spirit. Books like this one help the human spirit so that enjoyment of life and success can prevail.

Chapter One

The Role Of Neurpsychological Assessment in the Diagnosis and Treatment of Learning Disabilities in Adults

Sharon L. Zimmerman, Ph.D.

Sharon L. Zimmerman, Ph.D., is a clinical neuropsychologist in private practice in Cambridge, Massachusetts.

> *Said the Mock Turtle angrily: "Really you are very dull!"*
> *"You ought to be ashamed of yourself for asking*
> *such a simple question," added the Gryphon.*
> *And then they both sat silent and looked at poor Alice*
> *who felt ready to sink into the earth*
> (Lewis Carroll, *Alice's Adventures in Wonderland*).

An adult with a learning disability (LD) is likely to find Alice's experience distressingly familiar. While it is unlikely that Lewis Carroll meant to imply that Alice had a learning disability, this passage does eloquently describe an experience that most adults with learning disabilities have encountered repeatedly throughout their lives.

Since the 1970's, researchers have demonstrated that a learning disability persists into adulthood and may be permanent (Kaplan and Schacter, 1991; Spreen, 1989; Vogel, 1989). In a survey of 133 adults of above average intelligence who were diagnosed with learning disabilities as children, even those individuals with advanced degrees who had been highly successful in their careers indicated that the learning problems experienced during childhood continued into adulthood (Gerber, et al., 1990).

Unfortunately, many people with learning disabilities manage to graduate from high school without having a complete evaluation, or a formal diagnosis. For some adults, this is because they were in school at a time or in a geographical area where there was an incomplete awareness of a learning disability, or because there were insufficient resources available for assessment and treatment. In other cases, the individuals may be of above average intellectual ability and independently developed strategies to compensate for their learning disability. While academic achievement was lower than their true potential, learning was not so significantly impaired that the problem demanded attention. Instead, many of these adults report that they simply learned to cope with frustration, a vague sense that learning was more difficult than it should be and intermittent concern about being "stupid." Adults who have never been evaluated for LD but have struggled with learning in traditional academic settings sometimes seek an evaluation when their learning problems become more evident due to increased challenges in either the academic environment (e.g., college) or in vocational pursuits. Alternatively, as knowledge about learning disabilities in adults has become more universal, the formal, comprehensive evaluation of adult learning disabilities has become more available and more acceptable.

This chapter will discuss the role of neuropsychological assessment in the comprehensive evaluation of adult LD. After briefly reviewing the definition of a learning disability, the assumptions behind neuropsychological techniques and the purpose of the neuropsychological assessment will be discussed, as they pertain to the evaluation of adult LD. The scope of a typical neuropsychological examination will be outlined, including a description of testing procedures and some of the tests frequently employed. Finally, neuropsychological test data from a case of a 42-year-old man with a previously undiagnosed language learning disability, will be presented and discussed.

A Neuropsychological Understanding of LD and its Assessment

In 1989, the Joint Commission on Learning Disabilities established a widely accepted definition of learning disabilities. According to this definition, learning disabilities are a heterogeneous group of disorders involving a significant difficulty in the acquisition and/or use of one or more of the basic psychological processes involved in understanding or in using language (listening or speaking), reading, writing, reasoning and thinking, or mathematical ability. Individuals with learning disabilities are of average to above average intelligence (i.e., learning difficulties are not due to mental retardation). The learning problem is manifested in a significant discrepancy between aptitude and achievement. Although it may co-exist with motor or sensory handicaps, it is not solely attributable to them. This definition indicated that a learning disability was intrinsic to the individual, was presumed to be due to CNS (central nervous system) dysfunction and could occur across the lifespan.

This is an extremely comprehensive and useful definition. However, a neuropsychological understanding of LD includes additional components. A neuropsychologist assumes; 1) brain systems are specialized for different types of information processing, 2) these systems function both autonomously and converge, and 3) it is possible to localize systems to particular areas of the CNS (Pennington, 1991). For example, the brain structure (or physiological activity) of an adult who describes a lifelong difficulty with reading (dyslexia) is presumed to be different than the brain structure of an adult who has always struggled to pay attention, finish projects and think before acting. Further, a comprehensive neuropsychological understanding of LD requires the identification and functional definition of these localized brain systems. The literature has described a number of different typologies for classifying these functional systems (cf., Gardner, 1983; Rourke, 1985; Pennington, 1991; Gaddes and Edgell, 1994). There is some variation in these classification models, but most do refer, at some level, to brain systems mediating language abilities, visuospatial abilities, social cognition, executive functioning (selective attention, problem-solving, planning/organizational skills), motor functioning, memory, and mathematical ability.

A comprehensive neuropsychological evaluation is designed to assess each of these different domains of cognitive functioning. A battery of tests provides a standardized method for obtaining a systematic sample of behavior in a reasonable amount of time. Using data from these tests, it is possible to characterize the functioning of an individual's brain. Thus, neuropsychological assessment provides a functional picture of the brain, and can be considered a "functional CT scan". In addition, the assumed relationship between CNS structure and behavior, described above, enables the neuropsychologist to make inferences about the integrity of the brain or brain systems. It is presumed that the neurobehavioral measurement of cognitive processes has neurological validity and correlates to actual brain structures and/or activity (Fennell, 1995).

The Neuropsychological Evaluation

There are numerous circumstances that may prompt an adult to seek a neuropsychological evaluation of a possible learning disability. The academic challenges of college or graduate school often make learning problems more salient than they were in high school. An individual may experience job difficulties that are incongruent with his or her apparent level of ability. An adult may be thinking about returning to school, or about a career change. Often when a child is diagnosed with a learning disability (due to school difficulties), the parent recognizes similarities in his or her own cognitive style or history and decides to investigate the possibility that he or she has been struggling with a previously unidentified LD. In all cases, the first step is contacting a neuropsychologist and arranging a consultation. Possible referral sources include physicians, mental health professionals, school personnel or local and national advocacy groups for individuals with learning disabilities.

Neuropsychological evaluations can be time consuming, and costly. A comprehensive evaluation typically involves 4 to 8 hours of actual testing time, accomplished over the course of 1 to 3 separate testing sessions. Then, the neuropsychologist must score and interpret the test data and prepare a written report. In addition to the written record, the neuropsychologist will usually arrange a follow-up session to discuss results and recommendations and answer questions. The actual cost of the evaluation will then depend on the hourly rate for neuropsychological services in a particular geographical area. Some health insurance policies cover all or part of a neuropsychological evaluation. Some plans subsume these services under the mental health benefits. Others cover them with neurological services, under the medical benefit. If financial resources are limited, *and* the adult is interested only in addressing the question of a particular diagnosis or the characterization of a specific aspect of his or her learning style, an abbreviated battery may be appropriate. However, because learning disabilities are identified by comparing specific aspects of cognitive functioning to overall intellectual ability and to each other, a comprehensive evaluation is often necessary in order to arrive at a complete, accurate diagnosis.

A clinical interview comprises the first part of the neuropsychological evaluation. History is obtained from the individual seeking assessment, as well as from any available medical or academic records. Often, other significant people (e.g., spouse or partner, parents, siblings) can provide important additional information and therefore are included in part of the initial interview. The clinical interview usually begins with a discussion of the "presenting problem;" i.e., the reason precipitating the evaluation. Early developmental history is reviewed, if available. This includes questions about mother's pregnancy, labor and delivery, and achievement of early developmental milestones. Academic history is obtained. The neuropsychologist will ask about early reading experiences, mathematical skills, ability to concentrate, behavior problems, test-taking experiences, and grades. The highest level of education completed will be recorded. The adult may be asked to request any previous testing. Vocational history will be compared to estimated level of ability. It will be determined if the individual has significant difficulties with particular aspects of job performance. The neuropsychologist will inquire about medical history and will focus on conditions known to affect cognitive functioning. Medical records may be requested. Specific questions are likely to relate to a history of head trauma, seizures or of unusually high fevers as a child. The adult will be asked specifically about a number of specific medical conditions. A longitudinal description of alcohol and substance use will be obtained. Any psychiatric history will be reviewed. Finally, the interviewer will ask about family history. Information about neurological, psychiatric, and some medical conditions in close blood relatives will be collected, in order to assess any possible genetic predisposition to LD or comorbid conditions.

The actual neuropsychological examination is scheduled after the clinical interview. As noted previously, a comprehensive evaluation samples behavior from each of the principal domains of cognitive functioning. A wide compendium of tests is available to the neuropsychologist for the measurement of these domains. In order to develop an accurate, reliable, and detailed description of an individual's cognitive functioning, multiple tests are administered in each domain (Fennell, 1995). Through training and experience, neuropsychologists usually develop their own standardized battery of tests, and then modify this battery for each individual, depending on referral question, history and test results. Table 1 lists some of the neuropsychological tests commonly used to assess the aspects of cognitive functioning covered by a comprehensive evaluation.

A comprehensive examination starts with the administration of a standardized test of overall intellectual ability. The Weschler Adult Intelligence Scale – Revised (WAIS-R) is often used for this purpose. This test yields three composite scores; Full Scale IQ, Verbal IQ,, and Performance IQ. In addition, analysis of subtest scores can provide information about an individual's factual knowledge of the environment, attention, concentration, language comprehension, knowledge of social convention, abstract reasoning ability, sequencing ability, and visuospatial skills.

A more detailed exploration of particular domains of cognitive functioning follows. Assessment of language measures comprehension of spoken language, reading comprehension, oral expressive language, including repetition, articulation, prosody, fluency, and naming, reading (ability to form phonemic blends of words and non-words), appreciation of grammar and syntax, vocabulary, and verbal abstract reasoning ability. Visuospatial perceptual and constructional abilities are tested. Memory testing compares verbal memory functioning to visual memory functioning. Different modalities of stimulus presentation are employed so the processing of oral material can be compared to the processing of written material, and single stimulus presentation can be compared to multiple stimuli presentation. Techniques have been designed so that problems at different stages of the recall process can be identified. For example, a problem with the absorption of new information is presumed to have a different etiology then a problem with retrieval, or actual retention. Clearly treatment of these problems are different. The neuropsychologist also attempts to discern strategies that an individual may employ to learn and remember new information. Assessment of attention also compares auditory tasks to visual tasks. Distractibility, sustained attention, and concentration are all examined. Tests of executive functioning appraise an individual's abstract reasoning ability, cognitive flexibility, planning, and organizational ability, problem-solving ability, sequencing ability, and impulsivity or capacity to delay action. Fine motor coordination and speed (including handwriting ability) are examined. Finally the level of knowledge of basic academic subjects (i.e., reading, spelling and mathematical ability) is determined.

The functional description of an individual's cognitive style obtained from neuropsychological data can then be used to arrive at a diagnosis of a particular subtype(s) of LD. The data is examined to identify relative strengths and weaknesses in different aspects of cognition, and is also compared to normative data. This information is used to construct a profile of an individual's cognitive style, relative to his or her age peers. From this pattern of findings, the neuropsychologist can make inferences about the involvement of specific CNS regions or systems. Neuropsychological assessment is a particularly useful component of the assessment of learning disabilities because the detailed description of the individual's cognitive strengths and weaknesses available from the evaluation, allows the neuropsychologist to make explicit, concrete recommendations. Adults often have questions about how their learning style affects daily functioning. Suggestions for ameliorating learning may involve the proposal of environmental manipulations. Alternatively, specific strategies designed to build on cognitive strengths or compensate for areas of relative deficit may be outlined. Results can be interpreted in the context of questions the adult has posed regarding academic or vocational direction. Referrals for additional evaluation or intervention with a specialist in neurology, psychopharmacology, or psychoeducational counseling potentially provide additional sources of assistance and guidance.

The Case of Paul B.

Paul B. was 42-years-old when he first consulted a psychiatrist. His son had recently been diagnosed with Attention Deficit Hyperactivity Disorder (ADHD). Mr. B felt that he had many of the same characteristics as his son. Both he and his wife were especially con-

cerned about his "hot" temper. They wondered if this was a manifesta-
tion of ADHD that would be amenable to treatment with medication.

Mr. B. reported a history of poor school performance since elementary school. He had the most difficulty with reading and English.
He did graduate from high school, but still found reading problematic.
For example, as a deacon in his church, he had been asked to read in
front of the congregation, but always declined this honor, because he
was too embarrassed. Professionally, Mr. B. had been fairly successful,
although he had not been able to advance to the full extent of his talents
because he avoided written promotional exams. He had only a few
friends, but reported being generally satisfied by the companionship
provided by his family. He was therefore especially concerned when his
"hot" temper disrupted his home life.

Mr. B denied any history of depression, although he did admit to
"feeling down" for approximately six months after his mother died.
According to his wife, he became even more irritable, and "hot tem-
pered" during that time. He did admit to long-standing feelings of low
self-esteem which he attributed to his academic experiences. His wife
described him as chronically and characteristically "pessimistic."

There was no history of any head trauma or of any alcohol or
substance abuse. His medical history was noncontributory. His early
developmental history was unremarkable. Other than the recent diagnosis of ADHD in his son, there was no family history of either neurological or psychiatric disorders in family members.

As part of his psychiatric evaluation, Mr. B. was referred for neuropsychological testing. Test data is reported in Table 2.

Case Discussion

Testing revealed intact basic language skills (speech, comprehension, fluency), good visuospatial abilities, mild deficits in verbal memory, with better preservation of visual memory, intact executive functioning skills (including sequencing ability, problem-solving, abstract reasoning ability, and planning/organizational ability), and normal cognitive
and psychomotor speed. Mr. B's performance on one test of visual attention was slightly below average (Random Letter Cancellation Test), but
other measures of visual attention and auditory attention were all within
the average range. This was consistent with his average IQ. Thus, testing
provided little support for a diagnosis of ADHD. However, there was
clear evidence of a profound learning disability affecting reading,

spelling, and to a lesser extent mathematical ability. His WRAT-R achievement test scores were significantly below what would have been expected, given his average IQ. It may be hypothesized that the deficits observed in verbal memory functioning were a result of Mr. B's language-based learning disability. In fact, given the severity of his LD, his academic and vocational accomplishments were quite remarkable. His chronic pessimism, low self-esteem, and irritability ("hot-temper") were understood as a reaction to chronic experiences of failure and frustration associated with his previously undiagnosed learning disability.

Mr. B. was somewhat disappointed that there was no medication available to ameliorate his learning difficulties. However, he did find the definitive diagnosis of a language-based learning disability immensely relieving. He was referred to a local reading disorders clinic for tutoring. He was strongly encouraged to postpone his next professional examination until he had the opportunity to study the preparatory materials with his reading tutor. It was suggested that he investigate the possibility of his eligibility for an untimed or extended time exam. He was referred to a local chapter of an organization for individuals with LD for general information and support groups. Finally, it was recommended that he and his wife arrange for a short course of psychoeducational counseling so that they could learn to manage some of the interpersonal consequences of Mr. B.'s learning disability.

Table 1

A Sample of Neuropsychological Tests Used in Assessment of Cognitive Functioning

Intelligence
   Weschler Adult Intelligence Scale-Revised (WAIS-R)
Achievement
   Wide Range Achievement Test - 3 (WRAT-3)
   Reading, Spelling, Arithmetic
   Woodcock Johnson Battery
   Reading, Mathematics, Written Language, Knowledge, Skills
Language
   Boston Naming Test
   Controlled Word Association Test
   Vocabulary subtest of WAIS-R

Visuospatial Ability

Benton Judgment of Line Orientation
Block Design subtest of WAIS-R
Hooper Visual Organization Test
Rey Osterrieth Complex Figure (Copy)

Memory

Rey Auditory Verbal Learning Test
Rey Osterreith Complex Figure (Recall)
Ten-Word-Five-Trial Verbal Learning Test
Wechsler Memory Scale - Revised (WMS-R)

Attention

Connors Continuous Performance Test
Digit Span subtest of WAIS-R
Digit Span subtest of WMS-R
Picture Completion subtest of WAIS-R
Random Letter Cancellation Test
Test of Variability of Attention
Visual Span subtest of WMS-R

Executive Functioning

Halstead Categories Test
Rey Osterreith Complex Figure (Copy)
Similarities subtest of WAIS-R
Stroop Color Word Test
Trail Making Test
Wisconsin Card Sorting Test

Motor Functioning

Digit Symbol subtest of WAIS-R (psychomotor speed)
Finger Oscillation Test
Purdue Pegboard

Table 2
Test Data Summary

WAIS-R   FIQ = 101   VIQ = 100   PIQ = 102   (Mean = 100, SD = 15)

Verbal Subtests		**Performance Subtests**	
Information	10	Picture Completion	10
Digit Span	8	Picture Arrangement	9
Vocabulary	11	Block Design	9
Arithmetic	11	Object Assembly	10
Comprehension	11	Digit Symbol	10
Similarities	10		

(Subtest Mean = 10, SD = 3)

Achievement Tests - Wide Range Achievement Test - Revised

	Score	%ile	Grade Equivalent
Reading	74	4	7
Spelling	68	2	4
Arithmetic	93	32	9

(Mean =100, SD = 15)

Language Functioning
Boston Naming Test (Abbreviated)   15/15
Controlled Word Association Test   43 Words (Mean = 49, SD = 6)

Visuospatial Functioning
Rey Osterreith Complex Figure   34/36 (Mean = 33/36, SD = 6)
Hooper Visual Organization Test   24/30 (Mean = 26, SD = 4)

Memory Functioning
Rey Osterreith Complex Figure - Recall 15/36 (Mean – 19/36, SD = 7)
Ten Word -Five Trial Verbal Learning Test   7/10 Immediate 2/10 Delay
                                             18/20 Recognition

Executive Functioning
Stroop Color-Word Test   T Score = 43   (Mean T score = 50)
Trail Making Test   Form A = 40 seconds (25 %ile)
                         Form B = 55 seconds (75 %ile)
Random Letter Cancellation Test   5/60 misses, 75 seconds
Rey Osterreith Complex Figure   34/36 (Mean = 33/36, SD = 6)

Motor Functioning
Finger Oscillation Test   Right = 57   Left = 55   (Mean R = 43, L = 39)

Chapter Two

Understanding Your Learning Disability

Stephen Rothenberg, Psy.D.

Stephen Rothenberg, Psy.D., is a clinical psychologist in private practice in Framingham and Holliston, Mass. He is the host of the video, "Stop and Go Ahead with Success: An Integrated Approach to Helping Children Develop Social Skills" that won the 1999 Outstanding Media Production Award. He also serves on the board of directors of the Learning Disabilities Association of Massachusetts.

Understanding the Stages of Acceptance

Author of the seminal work on the grieving process, *On Death and Dying* (McMillan Press, 1969), Elisabeth Kübler-Ross, identified stages of mourning related to the loss of a loved one. These stages can be applied to other kinds of losses as well, such as the loss of the "perfect self" and the acceptance of a learning disability. Understanding learning difficulties means working towards acceptance of these problems. By understanding one's limitations, an individual can discover how to compensate, achieve and celebrate his or her unique learning style. If someone can not accept that he has these difficulties, then he may be in denial. This can result in self-loathing and a tendency to compare oneself to others. If the person is struggling with learning and sees that others approach these same tasks with ease, he is going to have a negative self-concept. He may begin to think that he is "stupid," which may lead to low self-esteem, failure to try and further feelings of failure. A negative spiral of despair may result. However, if someone is taught to understand that although his learning-style difference may require more effort, this difference is what makes him a unique individual, then he can learn to value himself as a worthwhile individual. This is what we refer to as "self-acceptance."

Dealing with Denial

As adults, especially as previously undiagnosed adults with learning disabilities, a very common response to the problem is to deny that it is happening. An individual may hide these difficulties from others because he feels that having a learning disability is something that is shameful and "bad." It can be too painful to admit that "I have more trouble learning than others." He learns to blame others, such as teachers or bosses who are unreasonable, or he may say that people do not explain things clearly. If this happens over and over again, it becomes more and more difficult to explain it away as someone else's problem. Consequently, he learns to deny his difficulties. He may spend great amounts of effort hiding his disability so that no one will see his problems and he does not have to face them. This effort can be very draining, since it utilizes a great deal of energy.

After the Shock Comes Relief

When an individual reaches the point when he has to admit to himself that there is a problem, this can be a shock to the system, at least initially. He can no longer pretend that there is nothing wrong. It's similar to someone not wanting to admit that the person he loved has died. The recognition of a learning disability is admitting that the perfect person he hoped to be does not exist. As adults, we relinquish our wish for a perfect self. As adults with learning disabilities, this can be an arduous task, but when the shock wears off, in it's place can come a feeling of great relief. It can be a heavy burden for an individual to sense that something is wrong throughout his life – to have that nagging fear that he is stupid.

Addressing the Anger

Once the shock wears off, the individual with learning disabilities may find that he is angry. He may think about times that he did not receive the help he badly needed. He may think of people who might have helped but, for whatever reason, did not. He may feel "robbed" of the support that he might have had if others had recognized his problems earlier. An individual may feel enraged because others have misinterpreted his difficulties as laziness or emotional problems. When it is determined that there is a real neurological reason for the difficulties, he may, for the first time, feel entitled to his anger. There also can be self-directed anger because he did not acknowledge his learning problems sooner. There can be rage directed towards whatever or whomever he thinks may be responsible for the learning disabilities in the first place – a feeling of "Why me?"

Just as it is critical to address feelings of denial so that the process or mourning can begin, it also is important to address the anger so that it does not become a crippling force. If an individual with a learning disability becomes enmeshed with blaming or self-pity, he robs himself of the possibility of moving forward. Once the rage is addressed, he is often left with a feeling of profound sadness.

Feeling the Sadness

When an adult with learning problems has worked through the anger, he can begin to address the sense of loss. It is a difficult loss to realize the loss of the idealized self – the self that was supposed to be. We all have dreams and images of ourselves as we develop emotionally and cognitively that can help, in a constructive manner, to drive us toward various goals. Having to give up certain images of the self and dreams that we have had in order to bring them more in line with reality is something that everyone faces as they become adults. An adult with a learning disability often will be faced with limitations that others may not experience.

I see one young man in psychotherapy who has spent many hours coming to terms with the loss of certain dreams. He had been depressed for a long time, in part because he felt like a failure. He had decided that, if he could not reach those dreams, then he and his life were nothing. Through therapy, he is beginning to see that, as he gives up some of his hard-held dreams, he has new dreams to pursue. These new dreams may not be as grand as his previous dreams, but they are worthwhile nonetheless. Often, there can be great regret at the opportunities that were missed or the path that cannot be pursued. With the mourning of these losses, certain paths may indeed be closed. At the same time, it is possible to become aware of the many roads that are still available.

Gaining Self-Confidence Through Acceptance

As an individual with learning disabilities has progresses through this mourning process, he is more likely to have a balanced and integrated view of himself. Emotional energy is no longer as connected to denial, anger and sadness. The individual has more resources available to pursue realistic and valuable goals. Acceptance also has an important impact upon self-esteem. An individual's self-concept will improve when he is able to look at all parts of himself and feel that he is "O.K." He is not as prone to feelings of low self-esteem or depression, if he is able to assess himself accurately.

If an individual has not accepted an accurate image of his strengths and weaknesses, then it is likely that he continually will have the feeling that he has failed or live in fear that others might discover the truth about his "incompetence." When he accepts his particular combination of personal strengths and weaknesses, then he is able to accept failure as just an instance where "I was unable to do something the way I wished," rather than "Look, this proves that I am a failure." He can gain self-confidence since he doesn't have to hide what he can't do and be proud of what he can do.

Getting What You Need, By Knowing What You Have

In order to have an accurate and balanced view of an individual's cognitive strengths and weaknesses, it is often helpful to seek a psychoeducational or neuropsychological evaluation By doing so, an individual can get a better understanding of his learning style, such as why learning about math comes so easily and reading is such a chore. Clinicians can assemble a cognitive picture of his strengths and weaknesses They also can teach strategies – "tricks" – to help the adult learn to compensate for his weaknesses in learning. Having a "picture" that makes sense, helps that person feel better about himself. Consequently, he is in a better position to acquire the skills he needs to be successful in a particular field of endeavor. He also is less likely to label himself as *dumb* or *stupid*.

When I work with an individual with learning disabilities in psychotherapy, we establish two important goals: (1) to learn about his strengths and weaknesses and (2) to become an advocate for himself. When an individual does not have a sense of what he might need in school and/or in the workplace, he can flounder, and it is less likely that he will get what he needs to succeed. When he can go to school or work and have a good sense of what it takes to be successful, he is more likely to do so. Prior to understanding what the learning problems are, an individual with learning disabilities can head in many different directions, wasting valuable time and effort. When he learns what the problems are and what can be done, then he has a "compass" to guide him and give him a clearer sense of direction.

Seeking Appropriate Emotional Help

Individual counseling or psychotherapy can be very helpful in addressing issues of self-esteem, depression, anxiety and goals clarification, among others. Since many individuals with learning disabilities also struggle with depression and/or anxiety at some time, it can be quite helpful to seek a consultation with a mental health professional.

> *Tim, a 30-year-old man, came into therapy following an incident with the law. He had average intelligence, could not read or write, was anxious a lot of the time (and drank to cope with his anxiety) and had extremely low self esteem. After he came in*

for therapy, we realized that, among other problems, he had previously undetected learning disabilities. Through the combination of an educational evaluation, tutoring and psychotherapy, he was able to understand his learning difficulties, realize how they had affected his life and to feel better about himself. He was able to increase his reading level, become more confident and he eventually reached a position of some responsibility in his union.

In the above example, Tim's undetected learning problems resulted in secondary emotional difficulties that were addressed through psychotherapy. Learning disabilities themselves, unless they are learning problems that are secondary to emotional difficulties, are not usually the direct focus of counseling or psychotherapy. Sometimes feeling depressed or anxious can be the result of struggling with learning disabilities. In a number of publications, depression and anxiety are referred to as "comorbid disorders." This means that anxiety and depression can coexist along with learning disabilities. It is not necessary to sort out which led to which. It is more important to get help for each area involved.

Finding Support Groups and Group Therapy

There are various support groups available for adults with learning disabilities. Some of these support groups focus upon the following:
• learning disabilities and work;
• learning disabilities and school; and
• learning disabilities and self-esteem.

Support groups allow people with similar problems to come together periodically to give each other mutual support and share resources. Groups can be very helpful because they provide an opportunity for people to be with others who have similar types of experiences. In this way, group "members" do not feel as alone or ashamed of their challenges. They can receive affirmation of their feelings and realize that what they are feeling is "normal." Support groups also offer a sense of hope for those involved. Individuals can learn from others who have been able to face and cope with various challenges. The group can offer a safe haven to draw strength from and to address whatever issues present themselves. Most importantly, individuals can learn to become assertive and effective advocates for themselves.

There may be more than one support group related to an individual's needs. Be selective in choosing a group. Each support group will develop its own "character" that reflects a unique mixture of individuals. One group may not be a good match, while another may "feel" just right. Look for a group where there are other individuals with similar issues. Listen to discussions over two to three meetings to see if you identify with what is being discussed. If not, it might mean that you should find a group that is more compatible with your needs.

There are different types of support groups. Some support groups are *self-help groups.* This means that the group is run by and for people with learning disabilities. There is no designated professional leader in these groups. An individual who joins the group shares his or her experiences with others and talks about what has and has not been effective.

Some self-help groups have been very successful without a professional leader (AA support groups, for example). There are also times within any group when very strong emotional reactions arise and/or complicated dynamics within the group may occur and may make it difficult for group members to manage on their own. A professionally led support group can offer more containment and safety under these circumstances. These groups differ from the self-help groups in that a professional leads the discussion. They function in a manner similar to the self-help group. Various topics are covered, resources are shared and support is available among group members. Your local learning disabilities association should be aware of the various support groups in your area.

Considering Psychotherapy Groups

Psychotherapy groups are helpful when an individual wants to work on problems that often accompany learning disabilities, especially those that stem from difficulty in interpersonal relationships. A psychotherapy group is one led by a professional. The purpose of the group is to alleviate certain problems (such as anxiety or depression) or to help compensate for a deficit (such as a social skills deficit).

An individual with learning disabilities also may experience significant difficulties in navigating the social world. He or she may have difficulty with their co-workers, bosses or people in close personal relationships. There is no known cause for these social difficulties. Some have problems reading social cues. Others may be able to read the cues but may have more difficulty executing the appropriate response. Whatever the problem in social functioning, group psychotherapy can offer help. In the context of a safe, accepting atmosphere, people with similar problems can practice new, more effective ways of relating. They are then in a better position to try out these new ways in their larger, social world.

Having a learning disability can be a tough challenge, but it is made easier when an individual is able to share his difficulties and successes with others. These groups provide strength and allow the individual to develop the inner resources to fall back upon when times are hard.

Finding a Therapist

When seeking a therapist, it is important to find someone with whom you feel comfortable, and who is equipped to understand your important thoughts and feelings. At first, you may feel uncomfortable and quite anxious. This is to be expected. You should feel that the therapist shows empathy for your difficulties and is competent. Seek a therapist who has particular expertise in helping people who have learning disabilities. This expertise makes it more likely that the therapist will have an understanding of with what an adult with learning disabilities has to cope. Your local learning disabilities association will most likely have a list of licensed professionals in your area who help adults with learning disabilities.

Remember that you are not only a potential client but a consumer as well. Feel free to ask the therapist questions about his or her credentials and experience. A good therapist should be open to answering these questions. Be cautious of therapists who comes across as overly defensive or impatient with these kinds of inquiries.

The therapist will most likely want to know your background. This will include your learning and medical history, as well as family background and relationship history. Following the initial evaluation (which can take from one to three sessions), you and your therapist will formulate a "treatment plan." Ideally, you would formulate goals for therapy upon which both you and your therapist agree. These goals should be clear and make sense. It is difficult to say exactly how long a given therapy will take, but your therapist should be able to give you an idea about whether therapy will be short or longer term. It will be helpful to "check in" with your therapist periodically to talk about how you are progressing toward your specified goals.

Lifetime Management for Success

Chapter Three

The Impact of Learning Disabilities on Adult Social Relationships

Jerome J. Schultz, Ph.D.

Jerome J. Schultz, Ph.D., is a clinical neuropsychologist in private practice in Wellesley Hills, Massachusetts. Dr. Schultz is the clinical director at the Learning Lab @ at Lesley College in Cambridge, Massachusetts. He also serves as vice president of the board of the directors of the Learning Disabilities Association of Massachusetts. He is the host of several videos: "Meeting with Success: Tips for a Successful IEP," winner of the 1999 Outstanding Media Production Award and the award-winning "Einstein & Me: Talking About Learning Disabilities."

If you were in school before 1978, the year that Public Law 94-142, the "Education For All Handicapped Children Act" became federal law, it's quite possible that you had a learning disability that was either not diagnosed, misdiagnosed, misunderstood, or mismanaged. As a result, you might have been one of the thousands of kids who grew up having difficulties in school who wondered, "What's wrong with me?"

Today, we know that early and accurate diagnosis, followed by appropriate intervention of learning disabilities can lead to better self-understanding and more successful academic, social, and vocational experiences. However, many individuals whose learning disabilities were *not* correctly identified grew up feeling confused, stupid, rejected, and dejected.

Unfortunately, the difficulties and the feelings of many individuals with learning disabilities were not traded in for the diploma they received at graduation. Too often these feelings were carried into adult life. The consequences of having a misunderstood learning disability as a child are different for each person, although there are some typical responses. Some people faced with early learning difficulties respond by "getting tough" and doing battle with every challenge that comes along. Others lack the supports to help them combat the chronic failure and, as a result, develop self-concepts that are built on shaky foundations. Whether they grow up with a feeling of "I must" or "I can't," the learning disability itself, as well as its emotional consequences, continue to have an impact on their adult life.

Since childhood relationships with family, friends, and teachers shape adult interactions, negative reactions from important people may have a damaging effect on the self-concept of young children or on how they feel about themselves and their abilities. If during childhood, individuals with learning disabilities were encouraged by supportive parents or teachers to develop what noted child psychologist Robert Brooks, Ph.D., refers to as "islands of competence" – things they did well that helped them feel good about themselves – this may offset some of the negative experiences. If not, they may go through life with a defeatist attitude.

Many people lead successful and happy lives even though they have a learning disability. They hold important jobs, have successful careers and some despite, or maybe because of their learning disability even become famous. Have you ever heard of Albert Einstein, Cher, Nelson Rockefeller or Tom Cruise? The following traits do not describe a particular individual, but they point out behaviors that *some* individuals with learning disabilities exhibit; few people exhibit all or a majority of these traits.

Learning Disabilities and Emotional Sensitivity or Vulnerability

Research has shown that learning disabilities may co-exist or exacerbate a variety of other conditions, such as Attention Deficit Hyperactivity Disorder (ADHD), anxiety disorders, obsessive-compulsive disorder, and depression. A learning disability may be accompanied by an exaggerated sense of worry or anxiety about little things. Difficulty letting go of ideas or worries may lead to more serious anxiety disorders or generate compulsive behaviors. Some people develop rituals or repetitive behaviors to protect themselves against making mistakes or to bring order to a disorganized life. Others are in such a state of worry that they become immobilized – unable to carry out normal activities of daily life.

Some adults may have learned to use their learning disabilities as an excuse for not doing what was expected of them. Teachers and parents may have used children's learning "problems" to excuse them or even exclude them from activities they were qualified to do. As adults with learning disabilities, they may have chosen a job with fewer demands so they wouldn't have to confront their problems. They may have chosen not to interact with some people in certain situations, especially when there is a chance that their learning disability will be "exposed." They may be afraid that someone will find out that they can't read or read well enough or that their difficulty spelling may overshadow their excellent verbal communication skills. This may cause them to avoid certain social or vocational situations.

A learning disability also may be associated with feelings of sadness or regret about things not done or goals not met. If these feelings persist for a long time, they may evolve into depression or make it more difficult to cope with a co-existing depression. It is important to point out that not everyone with a childhood learning disability grows up sad and lonely, but it is possible that a learning disability may have an impact on relationships with others. The way individuals view themselves effects how others see them, and most people do not consider chronic negativity or a sense of hopelessness as a positive attribute.

The Impact of a Learning Disability

The frustration, failure, or uncertainty that is often a part of learning disabilities can affect relationships. Instead of understanding that the individual with learning disabilities might be terrified of taking the risks involved in facing new challenges, people may see that person as lazy or unmotivated. Friends may grow intolerant of ambivalence or become annoyed by impulsivity, especially if that individual has ADHD, which often co-exists with learning disabilities. The following traits that are related to a learning difficulty may make activities of daily life more challenging than they are for people without a learning disability and do not endear them to others:
• trouble doing things on time;
• not being able to "read" other people's reactions;
• talking too much; or
• having a poor memory for dates, events, or promises made.

As a result of experiencing failure so many times in the past, an individual with learning disabilities may shy away from trying something even though he or she may be able to do it. Friends or a partner may not be able to understand her resistance and "hound" her to do something that may be anxiety provoking.

An adult with learning disabilities also may have difficulty getting involved in programs or support groups that might help him improve coping and interpersonal skills. He may be very wary of joining a group or taking a class because the memories of frustration, ridicule, and failure associated with past learning experiences in group situations are so vivid and painful. Since a learning disability is a life-long condition, he may wonder why things would be any better if he tried, yet again, to learn new things or new ways of interacting. As a result, he may limit his chances for personal growth. A partner or a spouse may not understand why he won't take a course or join a group, and may say, "If you really cared about me or our relationship, you would do this," leading to increased tension in the relationship.

Friends may become upset when they are unable to cheer up an individual with a learning disability or get them to take what seems like obvious steps to self-improvement. They may not understand that it may be more difficult for adults with learning disabilities to take action to help themselves. Some of the possible consequences of untreated learning disabilities, such as not showing up for appointments, not remembering commitments, and misunderstanding the meaning behind other people's words or actions also can have a detrimental impact on job security, as well as relationships. As a result, friends may not stick by the person with a learning disability or become resentful if they feel forced into staying in a relationship because the person having learning difficulties may seem so needy.

A Parent's Role

If a child with learning disabilities has a parent that has a learning disability, he or she is lucky – especially if that parent fared well. The parent is in a unique position to share stories about successes and frustrations (to the extent that *any* child listens to his parent's stories). He or she can tell the child how she dealt with teachers who didn't understand her learning disability or with peers who made fun of her. She can talk about things she did to help herself overcome the negative impact of having a learning disability. After all, that parent is living proof that a person can be successful despite the fact that she has a learning disability. If she had difficulties because of her disability, she also might be in a position to give the child advice about how *not* to handle certain situations.

If the child does *not* have a learning disability, he or she may grow tired of hearing about how the parent handled learning problems. Be aware of the child's reaction to these suggestions. Parents should keep disclosures about their learning disabilities brief and to the point, and stop when children are not willing to listen anymore. Children also may be very proud of parents because they overcame (and continue to overcome) the negative effects of having a learning disability, and this is a wonderful feeling when it happens. (Caution: parents may have to wait until their children are grown to hear about their proud feelings. Be patient!)

A Life of Problems or a Life of Solutions?

While we have a long way to go before the world is an ideal place for individuals with learning disabilities, there are many more resources and specialized opportunities for adults with learning disabilities than ever before. General Educational Development (GED) programs, colleges, and businesses are much more attentive to the needs of adults with learning disabilities who are returning to school or striving for success in the workplace. In addition, thanks to the significant public relations efforts of groups such as the Learning Disabilities Association of American (LDA), there is a greater level of understanding about learning disabilities among the general population. Mental health and medical professionals are better able to recognize learning disabilities and to differentiate them from other conditions that can make life challenging.

If the adult with a learning disability was passed over or minimized when he or she was younger, he may have a second chance at a very successful life. An evaluation of learning strengths and learning needs by a qualified psychologist can be a key to better self-understanding and can open the door for improved educational, vocational, and social opportunities. Most importantly, it is possible to educate friends or partners about why the person with learning difficulties does (or finds it hard to do) some things.

Some individuals with learning disabilities may not be able or ready to make big changes (or *any* changes) just yet. They may feel pretty good about how they are doing, despite the fact that they have a learning disability. Still others may wish for significant change. Some feel that there are areas of their lives that could use a little fine tuning or support. The following techniques to deal with learning disabilities are offered by a growing group of *successful* adults with these difficulties:

• **Increase your understanding of learning disabilities.** Consult a professional (e.g. your physician or a psychologist who works with adults who have learning disabilities) to confirm the nature and extent of your learning disability. Look for articles, journals, films, conferences, etc. that address issues pertinent to the lives of adults with learning disabilities, and learn as much as you can.

• **Practice self-advocacy: educate others about learning disabilities and how the LD impacts *you*.** Help spouses, partners, children, other relatives, employers, co-workers, employees, physicians, and other health-care professionals to learn more about learning disabilities by sharing materials you have found. Talk about your learning difficulties as an explanation and not as an excuse for certain behaviors, and let people know what you *can* do. Let them know how they can help you be productive.

• *Read* **the effect of your communication and behavior on other people and take active steps to correct a situation that may unravel.** Say to others, "I get the feeling that you haven't understood what I said. Let me try to say it another way." Or, "It seems like you are disappointed in me because I am not doing what you have suggested. Let me tell you why that is hard for me, and also what steps I am now taking to make progress in that area." If you can't do this alone, seek out the assistance of a third party, such as a counselor or family therapist who might be able to observe your interactions with another person and give you concrete feedback on your communication style and its effectiveness.

• **Identify supports that will help you address the challenges you face as an adult with learning disabilities.** Find other adults with learning disabilities who have found ways to cope successfully. Join support groups or attend special seminars that allow you to learn more about others and to share your successful experiences and suggestions with others. Don't be shy about seeking professional assistance, if you need more intensive support. Ask your physician or your local LDA for suggestions.

• **Take political action on behalf of all individuals with learning disabilities.** Support groups or activities that promote understanding about learning disabilities, such as the LDA and its state affiliates. Follow and support legislation such as the Americans with Disabilities Act (ADA) and the Individuals with Disabilities Education Act (IDEA), formerly the Education for all Handicapped Children Act. Keep your legislators informed about issues related to children and adults with learning disabilities.

• **Continue to grow and learn, personally and professionally.** As a result of greater understanding and new federal laws, schools and businesses are more likely now than in the past to offer supports and reasonable accommodations for adults with learning disabilities. If you encounter resistance or if you have questions about your rights, call your local LDA affiliate for guidance and support.

• **Be a role model for success.** Share your successful experiences with children and with other adults with learning disabilities. Inform them about steps they can take to better cope with their own learning disabilities.

There are many supports available to adults with learning disabilities, and there is good reason to be optimistic and hopeful that the future will be better than the past. Start a new venture or dust off an old goal. Take a small step *now* to help yourself or someone you care about who may have a learning disability.

Chapter Four

The Impact Of Learning Disabilities In the Workplace

Nancie Payne, M.S.

Nancie Payne, M.S., is the owner and senior consultant of Payne & Associates and the Northwest Center for the Advancement of Learning. Ms. Payne serves on the advisory board of the Learning Disabilities Association of America.

Individuals who have learning disabilities can face numerous challenges in the workplace if they are not prepared. Hidden and unseen by supervisors and co-workers, learning disabilities can significantly impact one's ability to obtain, maintain, and advance in a job or career. While not always predictable, many challenges can be anticipated by taking steps to effectively manage such impacts prior to the occurrence of potential difficulties. This advance thinking and planning, on the part of individuals who have learning disabilities, promotes positive actions that frequently minimize the impact of learning disabilities within the workplace. Thought should be given to the workplace environment, the essential functions required by the job, communication, and personal presentation skills needed for effective interaction with supervisors and co-workers, and possible or probable accommodations that are key to successful performance.

The Evolving Workplace

America has entered the "Third Wave Information Age" of the post-industrial era, according to author Alvin Tofler. The scientific and technological changes which are occurring are far more significant and unprecedented than have been recognized (Gingrich, 1995). The business focus has been dominated by three major factors: serving the customer, mastering the competition, and taking control of change (Hammer & Champy, 1993). Radical and dramatic changes have been occurring, re-shaping the American economy over the last 15 years. The multiple forces and variables of economic change generate challenges for prospective workers including those workers who have learning disabilities.

In the mid 1980's, economists began projecting major changes in the American economy and the context of work. By 1986, the National Alliance of Business, in the publication *Employment Policies: Looking to the Year 2000* projected that the greatest number of new job opportunities would be in occupations requiring some post-secondary education but not four-year degrees from colleges or universities. In the book *Worklife Visions* (1987) Hallett described work of the future as following a "twist-ing career path" (p. 14). He said, "The turbulence and uncertainty in the workplace could not be more clear. Everything is changing: every indus-try, every organization, every technology and every profession" (p. 15). In 1987, it was estimated that one out of every five people switched jobs each year and 1 out of every 15 switched careers (Hallett, 1987). In 1995, Unger wrote in *Management Review* that the average worker would change careers four to five times over the course of his or her work life. In 1988, Esther Friedman Schaeffer, Vice President for Policy for the National Alliance of Business stated: "There will be fewer sweat jobs and more (jobs) that require cognitive skills" (p. 3).

During this same period, there was a recognition that a learning disability was a life-long disorder. There was an emerging understanding of the characteristics in adults who have learning disabilities, and this revealed inconsistencies in performance in school and work due to the difficulty not only with cognitive functions including reading, writing, spelling, computing, and communicating orally, but also with higher-order thinking skills including multi-tasking, attending, organizing, problem solving, making generalizations, flexibility, and self-management. On the other hand, an assessment of the strengths of adults with learning disabilities showed a higher level of success when education and training was directly linked to authentic, hands-on learning environments in which the individual could maintain control of tasks and surroundings and additional learning time was provided.

There are limitations created by learning disabilities. These characteristics combined with the predicted strengths needed for success in the evolving workplace seem to contradict each other. The current and future workplace is dominated by increasing technological demands, more highly developed cognitive and higher-order thinking skills, fewer hands-on jobs, and rapid, constant workplace changes. Based on what is known about the characteristics and manifestations of learning disabilities, these changes have significant impact on individuals who have these disabilities and who are trying to prepare for and be productive in the workplace of the future.

Overall, the current work force profile characterizes a semi-skilled to unskilled labor pool in relationship to the industry projections and needs regarding future work opportunities. "Up-skilling" or continual education and training must become a way of life for every person who wishes to maintain consistent employment. However, too frequently individuals who have learning disabilities do not or are not able to access additional education or training to "re-tool" or "up-skill." This is due to a variety of reasons including the lack of varied learning environments, the need for modified training programs, and limited, available accommodations. Some individuals require the flexibility of a reduced work load in order to have a successful learning experience while others need individualized instruction and training support. More importantly, most adults who have learning disabilities need experiential, applied learning environments. In other words, doing is learning.

As we enter the twenty-first century, workers and prospective workers must be prepared to sustain employment in a contingency work force environment – taking his or her skills and providing short-term competencies and talents as an employee of contracted services. Workers and prospective workers will work in more small businesses than large corporations or they will develop their own businesses. Work will include flexible work schedules, multi-tasking, virtual offices, technology, and teams in entrepreneurial or intrapreneurial environments. Dr. Cal Crow, National Consultant, Center for Learning Connections, Highline Community College, Des Moines, Washington, made the following comment on a radio talk program, "Only the skilled will be well paid. Thus, each worker or prospective worker must acquire a range of skills which can be bundled and used in a job or career path" (1996).

Many individuals who have learning disabilities will find their niche in the new evolving economy. The ability to control one's workplace surroundings through flexible work schedules, multi-tasking, working in virtual offices, utilizing technology, and working on teams in entrepreneurial or intrapreneurial environments will produce the opportunity for success (Gerber, Ginsberg and Reiff, 1992). Information gathered about the characteristics and manifestations of adults who have learning disabilities suggests many do not know and/or cannot identify those specific strengths and attributes that are connected to job or career paths. Without this knowledge, it will be hard for the adult who has a learning disability to "bundle his or her skills" and associate those skills with a desired job or career. Based on economists and career professionals projections, the lack of knowledge of personal strengths and attributes coupled with under-developed skills may prevent adults who have learning disabilities access to livable wage jobs as well as wage progression.

Before education, training, or work-based upskilling or "skills bundling", can occur the necessary skills of the future workplace must be explored. A January, 1991 summary of findings from the Washington State Investment in Human Capital Study, entitled *Investing in Workforce Excellence* concluded that the greatest educational need of the future in order to compete and be productive in the workforce will be for all workers to have strong basic skills including the "new basic skills" (higher order thinking skills) involving judgement, critical thinking ability, and flexibility. Attributes and proficiencies necessary to compete must include creativity, innovation, critical thinking, problem solving, listening, speaking, personal management, self-esteem, motivation, goal-directed orientation, interpersonal, negotiating, knowledge of organizational productivity, and leadership skills.

Again, what is known and understood about the behaviors and manifestations of learning disabilities clearly displays inconsistent patterns in the application of knowledge, skills, and abilities. Sometimes, an individual who has a learning disability has well-developed basic skills but underdeveloped abilities in critical thinking, judgment, and flexibility. Sometimes the reverse is true. Frequently, individuals who have learning disabilities have high levels of creativity, innovation, and motivation which are offset by poorly or under-developed skills involving thinking and problem solving, listening and speaking, managing personal needs, self-esteem, goal-directed orientation, interpersonal and negotiation abilities, leadership, and organizational knowledge of productivity standards.

Koch (1994) raises concern that the significant workplace changes depicted here, coupled with the education and training required to maintain a livable and progressive wage may adversely impact the employability of individuals with disabilities, especially those who have learning disabilities. Given what is known about workers and prospective workers who have learning disabilities, the described changes and evolving differences in the workplace have and will continue to profoundly impact and affect those trying to secure, retain, and advance in jobs and careers.

Workers and prospective workers who have learning disabilities must be able recognize their strengths and attributes and connect them to the workplace. The question of "a good fit" is the most valuable question and the dialogue which ensues must identify all the elements that provide a clear pathway to the current and future workplace. These elements include: an understanding of the learning disability characteristics and manifestations, as well as the accommodations needed in various education, training and work environments; knowledge of strengths and abilities, as well as limitations created by the disability in various environments; identification of the individual's most productive processing style or learning characteristics; an understanding of and the ability to perform the essential functions required by specific jobs (including cognitive (basic) skills, as well as higher order thinking skills); the ability to communicate and effectively interact with supervisors and co-workers; and the ability to access education, training, and/or workplace skill development or enhancement specifying possible or probable accommodations necessary for skill acquisition and successful performance. Finally, workers and prospective workers who have learning disabilities must be able to competently self-evaluate and make adjustments as the future of work continues to change and evolve.

All this information begs the question: how will workers and prospective workers who have learning disabilities access these necessary skills? How will they gain the knowledge to bundle those skills and talents and match them with the job responsibilities and employer needs? Workers and prospective workers who have learning disabilities can access and utilize resources and services offered through regional one-stop career centers. At a career center, individuals will be able to access job search, referral, and placement assistance; training and education; testing, assessment, and counseling; support services such as fax machines, telephones, and computers for job searches; and assistance with individual benefits such as unemployment insurance and other related services. One-stop career centers will have access to additional resources and services to assist workers and prospective workers who have disabilities.

The message should be clear. In evaluating the past fifteen years, workplace changes can be described as constant and continuous. Over the last 10 years, these changes have resulted in the elimination of many jobs and careers – a significant "job shock" if one is not prepared. However, "job shock" is not a sign of decline, but a sign of progress (Dent, 1995. p. 17). The decline occurs when individuals who have learning disabilities do not anticipate workplace changes or develop personal plans to minimize the impact learning disabilities can have within the workplace. The true sign of progress is when individuals who have learning disabilities are effectively anticipating and planning for the changes in the workplace thereby controlling their environment rather than allowing the environment to control them.

Workplace Ups and Downs

This section will concentrate on the emotional and social effects learning disabilities have on employees or prospective employees both personally and on the job, as well as the impact felt by supervisors and co-workers. The scenarios present some opportunities to understand how knowing more about the learning disability, exploring how it impacts the work environment, and anticipating and planning might assist in improving performance and productivity.

• Scenario 1

Shirley is age 44 and a sales person in a hardware store. Her learning disability was not diagnosed until she was an adult, and it affects her visual processing, sequencing, auditory discrimination, and focus of attention. She said that she had difficulty concentrating at work because she is very distracted by background scenery. Her learning disability began to affect Shirley's job in the hardware store almost immediately. Her boss was upset about the reversal of letters and numbers when she shelved merchandise, when she input stock numbers into the computer, and when she transferred data from the telephone or computer to work orders.

Without accommodations, the impact of Shirley's learning disability on her job was significant. She often had to fix an order that she had filled incorrectly. Other sales people had difficulty finding stock that Shirley shelved in the wrong bins, and inventory control was difficult because of inaccuracies when she pulled orders and merchandise. In short, her productivity was very low, and she was costing the company money. More importantly, Shirley was not viewed by her supervisor as highly as other sales people because her supervisor could not understand why Shirley did not do her job right the first time. Although everyone makes a few mistakes, there was a limit. Because Shirley really wanted to do a better job, she tried working faster and working longer hours. Unfortunately, the result of her efforts did not improve her performance, but rather compounded issues. Working faster led to more mistakes; working longer hours led to being tired which also led to more mistakes. The other sales people began to complain about her mistakes and her boss continually emphasized the need for accuracy if she wanted to keep her job adding more stress and making matters worse instead of better. Clearly, without her disclosing and explaining the affect of her learning disability to her employer and without appropriate accommodations, Shirley's learning disability would continue to impact her employment.

• Scenario 2

Miguel is 43-years-old and was an equipment repair assistant for nine months until he was fired. He remembered being in special reading classes off and on in elementary school, and learning how to read enough to survive. Generally, he knew he could "do it," things just came slow. He got most of his jobs because he was always on time, had a good attitude, and was a hard worker. However, throughout this and other jobs he held, he encountered difficulties. Most recently, as an equipment repair assistant, he had difficulty finding the right manuals or repair update notices for the different models of equipment. He also had trouble estimating how long the repair would take and when the customer could pick up the equipment. Writing work orders and figuring parts/equipment costs, making change in a cash transaction, following oral directions, and communicating with co-workers was a challenge. Miguel really liked people, but he had a tendency to blurt out things or say things backwards and was quite sure he had offended many people. In fact, his ability to stay in a job usually depended on how much interaction with people was required.

Miguel was aware he had been diagnosed with hyperactivity as a child but did not realize his difficulties might also include a learning disability. Finally, when Miguel was tested for learning disabilities, he learned that he had difficulties with visual processing, short-term memory functions, and manual dexterity and fine-motor coordination, especially when writing, making change and – you guessed it – doing equipment repair work. How did Miguel's learning disabilities impact his work? Obviously, very seriously since he had lost a number of jobs. It also significantly affected his mental status. He was angry and felt overwhelmed and helpless. However, after he found out he had a learning disability, he began seeing a counselor and participating in an adult support group. The healing process now had begun, he started to rethink training and job opportunities. He felt that although nothing is perfect, with the knowledge and understanding of his disability, job or training opportunities that use his skills and abilities, and accommodations in work environments, surely things would get better.

• Scenario 3

Sophia is 39 and employed by a county health department as a medical evaluator. In her fourth month of a six-month probationary period, she experienced great difficulty performing specific aspects of her job, including extrapolating and analyzing data by using the county's computerized system and software. Additionally, she had trouble stating the extrapolated information clearly and concisely in written reports with appropriate conclusions and supporting charts and graphs. She felt if she did not receive help from somewhere, she would lose her job. She had been diagnosed with a learning disability prior to accepting this job but did not want to disclose this information to her supervisor, nor did she wish to tell her supervisor she was experiencing difficulty with specific tasks. Instead she accessed a computer training service as well as a private tutor and concentrated on the specific work skills she was having difficulty performing. Because she understood a great deal about her learning disability and the best methods for her to learn, she was able to concentrate on an individualized approach that accommodated her learning needs. She worked long hours before and after work, but managed to learn and successfully apply sequencing, critical thinking, and functional report writing skills without disclosure to her supervisor. Could she have done it alone? Probably not. Her learning disability could have had a significant impact on her work, but it did not because of her knowledge of how she learned best and her ability to access resources.

Personal Workplace Strategies

Everyday, somewhere, someone who has a learning disability is impacted by the workplace – and – everyday, somewhere, the workplace is impacted by an employee or prospective employee who has a learning disability. That impact can be a positive or a negative experience, depending on how one manages his or her learning disability within the environments and influences of the workplace. Supervisors and co-workers do not always have accurate information or perceptions about the reality of having a disability – especially a learning disability, and unfortunately, many adolescents and adults know very little about their learning disability.

Roper Starch Worldwide (1996) commissioned by the Emily Hall Tremaine Foundation conducted a nationwide study measuring public awareness and knowledge of learning disabilities. The study concluded that the American public's true ignorance of learning disabilities becomes abundantly clear when people were asked whether the following nine conditions: dyslexia, attention deficit disorder, attention deficit hyperactivity disorder, autism, mental retardation, blindness, deafness, slow learner, or other emotional disorders were associated with learning disabilities. The majority responded that all nine conditions were associated with learning disabilities. Sixty percent associated blindness with learning disabilities, 85 percent associated mental retardation with learning disabilities. This perception should assist in understanding why many co-workers and supervisors respond in unexpected ways when a learning disability is disclosed by an employee or prospective employee.

An important element of having success on the job emotionally and socially is finding a good fit. Gerber, Ginsberg and Reiff (1992) suggest a significant part of adaptability is making sure the environment, job tasks, and responsibilities, co-workers and other aspects of the workplace are aspects which promote the individual's skills and abilities. Learn to identify the negative job matches and try to avoid them.

Recognize and anticipate that when job changes or promotions are coming up that there will be differences, and that some or many accommodations that worked in the previous position may not work in the new position. Sometimes, an adjustment is needed. Two or three weeks after being on the job, identify the specific performance or evaluation criteria you will be measured against at the end of your probation period. Set up specific goals and objectives as well as identifying check points with your supervisor or co-workers to receive input about your improving performance.

It is a misconception to think, "When I get the job, things will be different and my learning disability won't affect my work." It's true that the job environment will be different which is exactly why an employee or a prospective employee should be doing frequent self-evaluations. Try to get weekly or monthly feedback from the supervisor and significant co-workers about performance and areas of improvement.

Some believe that once they disclose they have a learning disability, everyone will understand and accommodate. Recognize that the learning disability must be owned by the individual diagnosed with the disability – only you are responsible for total understanding. Others should respect your right to accommodations. While the impact of disclosing your learning disability may make you feel vulnerable, the same may be true of choosing not to disclose. Weigh your options carefully and prepare and create a plan. This will allow you to work through all your options and make decisions from a better base of knowledge.

Understand that being diagnosed with a learning disability does not remove or replace the knowledge, skills ,and abilities requirements, in any workplace. It is important to have the knowledge, skills, and abilities to perform the tasks of the job. Diagnosis provides a chance for accommodations to be put into place to allow an equal opportunity to compete and demonstrate knowledge, skills and abilities, without regard to the disability.

The following strategies may help you adjust in the workplace:
• Know what it means for you to have a learning disability. Everyone learns differently, approaches tasks using various methods, thinks and

responds with individualism. Understand yourself.

• Be able to explain your disability, and the accommodations you do or might need. Only you will be able to predict what will and will not work. Sometimes, there needs to be an element of trial and error or experimentation. Your supervisor or co-workers can give you suggestions and help identify possibilities, but you are the only person who can identify what will and will not work.

• It is not okay to use your learning disability as an excuse. There are times when accommodations are needed to perform. Asking for an accommodation is not an excuse, however, saying something can't be done or didn't get done because you have a learning disability may be perceived as an excuse. Learn to evaluate and ask for specific accommodations when needed. Some accommodations and strategies can be implemented without any assistance from co-workers or supervisors. Know what resources are available and how to access them.

• Try to look for the positive elements of every situation. Recognize the problem, identify a solution or method to remedy the problem, then concentrate on the positive aspects of implementing the solution or remedy. This approach will get you a lot further than consistently bringing up the negative aspects of the situation.

• Be in control of your learning process and task completion process. Remember, many times individuals who have learning disabilities are able to identify different, more effective methods to approach a task or solve a problem than their co-workers or team because they are innovative and creative thinkers.

• Access support systems. Talk to people outside your work environment who you respect and who are successful at their job (preferably outside your own workplace environment). Ask them to give you pointers, advice and assistance. Develop a professional relationship with that person. Join a support group. The way to improve and grow is to keep learning and understanding ourselves. Support from people who are in similar situations is an important element of creating success.

• Recognize the need for professional counseling. Try to find a counselor or therapist who understands learning disabilities and is knowledgeable about workplace relationships and interaction.

• Make a commitment to continuous, personal improvement. Upgrade and enhance your skills. Learn to work in teams, adapt to changes as quickly and easily as possible, and understand your relationship as an employee to the overall productivity of the company or business. Anticipate and plan.

• Take a communication class. Attend a lecture about learning styles, get a tape on improving self-esteem, and take a workshop on developing and maintaining relationships. Explore new environments and take up hobbies and interests. Diversify your activities to help reduce the stress of the job, managing accommodations, and maintaining working relationships. Take a break – learn to have fun.

• Work on and improve your social skills. You can improve upon your ability to socialize and interact effectively with friends, co-workers and supervisors. In the Learning Disability Association of America survey, *They Speak for Themselves* (1996), the respondents described that many times unemployment and loss of jobs more often resulted not so much from lack of specific work skills, but rather from inadequate social skills.

• Reduce your stress and learn to be mentally tough. Be good to your body and your mind. Practice good health habits, use laughter and humor effectively and visualize success (McLaughlin, Loehr & Simons, 1994).

Personal Presentation

Learn to be patient. Try to employ the "listen and think about it" method. Listen to the issue, situation or need and unless there is an obvious solution, ask if you can get back to the person the next day (preferably first thing in the morning). That way you have some time to think about the information presented. Check with others who may have encountered similar experiences and weigh your choices.

Many of us display feelings and emotions in a direct and obvious manner. Whatever is in the heart or mind comes out in the emotions or actions. Learn how to monitor and respond appropriately in work situations. "Those of us who work with and are part of this population must instill in each other that the quality of one's social relations begins with me" (Crawford, 1995).

Do what is fun and the rest will come. If you are not having fun and you cannot see yourself having fun in the foreseeable future, then evaluate why and change what needs to be changed. The only way to evaluate personal performance is to first recognize and understand your disability, assessing how it affects you, the job and you on the job. Secondly, if improvement is needed, map out a plan with action steps and time lines for accomplishments. Third, implement your plan. Fourth, evaluate how our plan is progressing and adjust as necessary.

People's expectations about the future influence the decisions they make today (Occupational Outlook Quarterly, U.S. Department of Labor, 1993). The most important decision any individual can make is to work for or start the right business. (Dent, 1995). Change reactions to responses.

Chapter Five

Legal Issues in Education and Work

Peter S. Latham, J.D.
Patricia H. Latham, J.D.

Peter S. Latham, J.D., and Patricia Horan Latham, J.D., are partners in the Washington, D.C. law firm Latham & Latham, founders and directors of the National Center for Law and Learning Disabilities, arbitrators for the American Arbitration Association, and authors of and contributors to many books on legal issues.

In this chapter, we will provide an overview of the legal rights of an individual with a learning disability (LD) and Attention Deficit Disorder (ADD) in postsecondary education and the workplace under the Americans with Disabilities Act of 1990 and the Rehabilitation Act of 1973. Discussion will include a legal rights overview, its application to postsecondary education, its application to the workplace, disclosure and documentation of the disability, confidentiality and advocacy – communication, negotiation, mediation, arbitration, and litigation.

A Legal Rights Overview

The rights of individuals with ADD/LD derive historically and logically from the Fifth and Fourteenth Amendments to the Constitution. The leading case for disability purposes is *Brown v. the Board of Education*, 347 U.S. 483 (1954). While Brown is best known for its racial classification holding, it also stands for the proposition that the equal right to an education is a fundamental human right. The court said the following:

> *In these days, it is doubtful that any child may reasonably be expected to succeed in life if he is denied the opportunity of an education. Such an opportunity, where the state has undertaken to provide it, is a right which must be made available to all on equal terms.* 347 U.S. 483, at 493.

In the years that followed Brown, the lower federal courts implemented the spirit of that ruling and extended the protections of that case to individuals with disabilities, initially in the public school systems. These fundamental rights are made specific by statutes. The following federal statutes confer rights on persons with disabilities in education and work:

• **The Americans with Disabilities Act of 1990 (ADA)** – This act prohibits discrimination against qualified persons with disabilities. The ADA applies to (1) employers with 15 or more employees (Title I), (2) all activities of state and local governments, including but not limited to employment and education such as public schools and colleges (Title II), and (3) virtually all places which offer goods and services to the public termed "places of public accommodation" such as private schools and colleges, except for religiously controlled schools. In addition, the ADA applies to employment by the Congress.

• **The Rehabilitation Act of 1973 (RA)** – This act made discrimination against individuals with disabilities unlawful in three areas: (1) employment by the executive branch of the federal government (2) employment by most federal government contractors and (3) activities which are funded by federal subsidies or grants. This latter category includes all public elementary and secondary schools and most postsecondary institutions. The statutory section which prohibits discrimination in grants and other forms of financial assistance was numbered § 504 in the original legislation. The RA is often referred to simply as "Section 504".

The courts have given the nondiscrimination provisions of § 504 a broad reach by finding the existence of federal financial support and funding in a range of circumstances. In *New York v. Mid Hudson Medical Group, P.C.* [1], the court found that § 504 applied because of Medicare/Medicaid receipts by doctors which the court held constituted federal financial assistance. In *Delmonte v. Florida Dep't. of Business & Prof. Regulation* [2], the court held that the Florida Department of Business Regulation was subject to the RA, because the department had "accepted training by several federal law enforcement agencies at no cost".

Establishing a Disability Under the ADA/RA

The RA/ADA, apply to any "individual with a disability" which includes one who has a physical or mental impairment which substantially limits one or more of that person's major life activities.[3] The term "mental impairment" includes "any mental or psychological disorder, such as mental retardation, organic brain syndrome, emotional or mental illness, and specific learning disabilities." [4] 29 CFR § 1613.702(b)(2). In order to obtain the protections of the ADA/RA, a person must establish that the ADA or RA applies and that he or she (1) is an individual with a disability, (2) is "otherwise qualified" and (3) was denied a job, education or other benefit "by reason" of that disability. The term "individual with a disability" includes individuals with LD and ADD who are substantially limited in a major life activity. Similarly covered are psychiatric disorders such as depression. Alcoholism is covered, but current illegal drug use is not. A recovering illegal drug user who has been drug free for a reasonable period may be covered.

A learning disability is expressly covered as an impairment. Attention deficit disorder is not expressly covered as an impairment but has been recognized as such in court cases and official pronouncements of the department of education. For example, in the Letter of Finding issued to Camdenton (MO) Parish RIII Sch Dist., OCR Docket No.

07931031; 20 IDELR 197 (April 30,1993), the Office for Civil Rights ruled when ADD substantially limits a major life activity, it is covered by the definition of disability.

In other words, qualified individuals with LD and ADD whose impairment substantially limits a major life activity may be covered by the ADA or RA. Coverage means that these individuals have a right to be free from discrimination in education and work. Specific application of these laws will be discussed in the sections below, including a review of accommodations that may be required in postsecondary education and workplace settings. These requirements apply to federal executive [5] and congressional branch employment [6], federal financial recipients [7], federal government contractors [8] and state and local governments. Also included are "places of public accommodation" – a term which includes private elementary, secondary and postsecondary educational institutions and most private employers.

Academic Adjustments and Reasonable Accommodations

Postsecondary students with learning disabilities and Attention Deficit Disorder are entitled to be treated in a non-discriminatory manner in postsecondary programs and activities, including recruitment, admission, academic programs and athletics. The right to be treated in a non-discriminatory manner may mean that a student is entitled to accommodations in order to make the program accessible. Accommodations may include extra time on tests, separate room to reduce distractions, use of a tape recorder in classes, notetakers, readers, books on tape, priority seating, and priority registration.

Postsecondary students who provide documentation of their disability and are qualified for the program are entitled to appropriate academic adjustments and auxiliary aids and services at no additional charge. However, there is no right to accommodations that would pose an undue burden for the institution such as a financial burden or a fundamental alteration in the nature of the program.

Reasonable accommodations are alterations in *non-essential* testing requirements,[9] the delivery of course materials[10] or job requirements[11] which will enable a child or adult with a disability to perform the *essential* or fundamental tasks involved. Modifications which would require alteration of the fundamental nature of a test, course of study or job or which would cause an undue hardship are not reasonable and are not required.[12]

The requirement for reasonable accommodation affects virtually all educational institutions (regardless of whether they are elementary, secondary or postsecondary) in three principal areas: 1) testing (for admissions, evaluation of academic performance and graduation), 2) the delivery of course materials, and 3) non-academic benefits of school or college life; e.g., sports, dormitory living, etc. The bases for these common requirements vary, depending on whether the educational institution is public or private, elementary or postsecondary.

Special education and services in *public* elementary and secondary education are governed primarily by the Individuals with Disabilities Education Act (IDEA).[13] The RA/ADA also apply, but in many cases their coverage is similar to the IDEA's coverage.[14] However, some children who may not qualify for special education under the IDEA may still qualify for accommodations and services under the RA. Accommodations in *private* elementary and secondary education are governed only by the RA/ADA. Postsecondary institutions, including colleges, graduate schools and institutions which prepare individuals to take or which administer entrance examinations and professional licensing examinations are governed by the RA and ADA.[15]

Examinations must be structured in such a way that their results "accurately reflect the individual's aptitude or achievement level or whatever other factors the examination purports to measure".[16] In general, entrance and other examinations may not reflect "the individual's impaired sensory, manual or speaking skills" unless 1) the purpose of the test is to measure those factors, and 2) the measurement of those factors has a valid educational purpose. Testing which relies on a single criterion is unlawful where that criterion can be shown to be an inaccurate predictor of performance, and the use of that criterion has no compelling justification.

The examinations are generally required to be modified a) "in the length of time permitted for completion" and b) in the "manner in which the examination is given."[17] Auxiliary aids and services must be provided. Modifications are not required where they will alter the fundamental nature of the course or pose an undue hardship. The U. S. Department of Education has stated that in making undue hardship determinations, the primary consideration will be the size and budget of the institution compared with the cost of the requested aids and not the amount of tuition paid by the student.[18]

An educational institution must provide equal access to classroom and other educational materials. This duty is described in the regulations as an obligation to provide auxiliary aids and services.[19] The auxiliary aids and services must "recognize individual communications needs" and must provide "contemporaneous communication" of the entire educational experience including class participation being offered. Their selection is to be primarily guided by a consultative process *with* the student and not just unilaterally by the institution.[20]

The following are some examples of court decisions on accommodations requested by postsecondary students:

• A medical student with a learning disability who has been provided many accommodations in class and on tests sues his medical school claiming that it had an obligation to provide him with examinations in a different format than multiple choice. Result: the student is not entitled to a test format other than multiple choice. See *Wynne v. Tufts University School of Medicine.* [21]

• A lawyer with a learning disability and Attention Deficit Disorder sues the bar examiners who have denied double time on the test and a private room. Result: the lawyer is entitled to the requested accommodations. See *Weintraub v. Board of Bar Examiners.* [22]

• A student with a learning disability requests triple time on a standardized test and has professional documentation supporting the request. The testing service categorically limits extended time to double time. Result: the student is entitled to an individual determination as to the appropriate amount of extended time and on the documentation submitted is entitled to triple time.

• A student with a learning disability is in the first year of college and wants to be provided accommodations but does not wish to sign up for the LD services program and pay the fee for that program. Result: the student may receive legally required accommodations at no additional charge. See *United States v. Board of Trustees for the University of Alabama,* [23] and *University of Arizona.*[24]

• A college offers a program for students with learning disabilities who are not qualified for admission to any regular programs of the college. The fee may be higher than the fee for the regular program. Result: the college may charge a separate and possibly higher fee for the special program because the student is not qualified for admission to the regular program. *Halasz v. University of New England.* [25]

How can a person with a learning disability or Attention Deficit Disorder who is in medical school or has graduated from law school be substantially limited in learning? The person may have studied assignment three times longer than classmates. However, when confronted with the absence of the accommodation of extra time, the person may fail.

In *Pazer v. New York State Board of Law Examiners,* [26] a candidate for the bar examination brought suit under Titles II and III of the ADA to obtain an injunction requiring the New York State Board of Law Examiners to provide him with 1) double time, 2) use of a computer with word processing, spell-checking and abbreviation expanding software, 3) permission to record the answers to multiple choice questions in his answer book, and 4) a testing location which would minimize distractions.

The court first considered the question of whether any person whose compensatory strategies for dealing with a learning disability enabled him to graduate from law school could be said to function below the average of the general population, and therefore to have a disability under the law. The court therefore found some merit to the argument that a disparity between inherent capacity and performance on a test may, in some circumstances, permit the inference that an individual has a learning disability, even though that individual's performance has met the standard of the ordinary person. [27] Having recognized the possibility that a law school graduate might nonetheless have a learning disability sufficiently severe to qualify as a disability under the ADA, the court found that the record in that particular case was insufficient to show the existence of a learning disability.

The Late Diagnosis: An Individual May Qualify

Some individuals with learning disabilities and Attention Deficit Disorder are not diagnosed until they are adults. In those cases, documentation is of key importance in establishing that the person currently has an impairment that substantially limits learning and that symptoms existed earlier that either had impact or were compensated for or accommodated officially or unofficially. Similar issues arise in the employment area.

Individuals who have LD and ADD that substantially limit a

major life activity are entitled to be free from discrimination in the workplace. The principles we have discussed also apply to employment, but their application is somewhat different.

In the employment setting, just as in the postsecondary setting, an impairment must substantially limit a major life activity before it can be considered a "disability" under the law. The major life activities are considered to be "caring for oneself, performing manual tasks, walking, seeing, hearing, speaking, breathing, learning, and working".[28] Note that the regulations provide that learning and working are major life activities, and that these are the ones that most concern us. However, working is treated differently from all other major life activities for purposes of considering whether an individual with an impairment is substantially limited. In order to determine whether a substantial limitation on working exists, the individual's impairment must bar him or her from significant *classes* of jobs, and not just a *particular* job. Only disabilities with the former (and broader) impact are considered to substantially limit working.

An impairment – to constitute a disability – must represent a substantial limitation to a major life activity. However, the list of major life activities contained in the federal regulations is (by its own admission) not exclusive. The Equal Employment Opportunity Commission (EEOC) has recently added thinking, concentrating and interacting with others to the list of major life activities its investigators will recognize. The EEOC's view is that "... major life activities include sitting, standing, lifting and mental and emotional processes such as thinking, concentrating and interacting with others." The explicit recognition is that particular "mental and emotional processes" are among the major life activities that may help to resolve the problem that is addressed in the EEOC's statement. An accomplished person in overall learning may nonetheless be impaired in the particular processes of concentrating or visual discrimination.

Under both the RA and ADA, an individual with a disability must be one who is "otherwise qualified." An otherwise qualified individual is one who, though possessed of a disability, would be eligible for the education, job or program benefit, with or without a reasonable accommodation. The institution or employer must either provide the accommodation or justify in detail the refusal to provide it. *Fitzgerald v. Green Valley Area Education Agency.* [29]

Note that in public elementary and secondary school, a student is presumed to be qualified for public education. Thus, it is not necessary to prove that the student is otherwise qualified. The basic prohibition of the RA/ADA is summarized by 28 CFR § 36.201 which prohibits discrimination by a "place of public accommodation" in the provision of "goods, services, facilities, privileges, advantages, or accommodations."

> *(a) Prohibition of discrimination. No individual shall be discriminated against on the basis of disability in the full and equal enjoyment of the goods, services, facilities, privileges, advantages, or accommodations of any place of public accommodation by any private entity who owns, leases (or leases to), or operates a place of public accommodation.* [30]

The outright denial of participation in education, occupations, professions and employment is, of course, prohibited.

Reasonable Accommodations in the Workplace

The requirement for reasonable accommodation generally applies in the workplace as well. Again, *non-essential* testing and job performance requirements must be modified. Modifications which would require fundamental job alterations or undue hardship are not required.

In *Beck v. University of Wisconsin*, No. 95-2479, January 26, 1996, the Seventh Circuit considered the case of a secretary who "suffered from osteoarthritis and depression" during the latter part of her employment. (She was employed as a Secretary from 1967-1993). Following a three month medical leave, she disclosed her disabilities and supported them with letters from her doctor. However, she refused to sign a release allowing the university to obtain further information from her doctor and provided no further information about her need for accommodations. The university refused to meet with her to discuss possible accommodations. Adjustment to her workload was the only accommodation specifically requested by the doctor and it was granted. Following another medical leave, the university offered the secretary her old job back, and when she insisted on another job, she was fired.

She brought suit under the ADA, lost in the trial court and appealed to the Seventh Circuit which affirmed. In doing so, the Seventh Circuit reasoned that the ADA and its regulations contemplate an interactive process to identify appropriate accommodations. The employer must provide information about its facilities and equipment, and the employee must provide information about his or her disability.

Once an employer knows of an employee's disability and the employee has requested reasonable accommodations, the ADA and its implementing regulations require that the parties engage in an interactive process to determine what precise accommodations are necessary. In this case, the interactive process broke down. The employer was left to guess what actions it should take, and the employee was left frustrated that her disability was seemingly not accommodated. Liability for failure to provide reasonable accommodations ensues only where the employer bears responsibility for the breakdown. But where, as here, the employer does not obstruct the process, but instead makes reasonable efforts both to communicate with the employee and provide accommodations based on the information it possessed, the ADA liability simply does not follow. Because the university was never able to obtain an adequate understanding of what action it should take, it cannot be held liable for failure to make "reasonable accommodations." The judgment is therefore affirmed.

Documentation of the disability is key to establishing eligibility. Ordinarily, documentation will be based upon history, testing, personal interview, and medical examination.

Under the RA and ADA, individuals with impairments which substantially limit a major life activity are considered individuals with disabilities. In order to obtain their protections, an individual may be required to document his/her disability. There are three basic elements to a proper disability documentation: 1) diagnosis, 2) impact evaluation, and 3) recommendations.

A *diagnosis* is what its name suggests: an authoritative opinion by one qualified to assert it, concluding that a specific disability is present. Legally speaking, that also establishes the existence of an impairment under the RA/ADA. Some courts appear to prefer diagnoses which refer to the *Diagnostic and Statistical Manual of Mental Disorders* published by the American Psychiatric Association. Now in its fourth edition, this book is referred to as DSM IV. [31]

An *impact evaluation* demonstrates how the diagnosed impairment affects the individual. Legally speaking, it must show that, in the individual case, the impairment substantially limits a major life activity, such as learning or working. *Recommendations* suggest reasonable accommodations appropriate for the individual.

How Much Testing is Enough?

How much testing and evaluation are enough? Determining how much is enough is a matter of professional judgment and depends upon what you want to do with the results. At one end of the spectrum is the individual who has sought testing to gain self-knowledge and treatment recommendations. In such a case, the amount of documentation is simply that which a responsible medical practitioner will require in order to make a diagnosis, prescribe medication and select appropriate additional treatment. At the other end of the spectrum is an individual with disabilities who has sought testing in connection with the assertion of a legal right. A school or employer might be resistant to the request for accommodations or services. Probably the best strategy is to proceed on the basis that the individual may one day desire to request accommodations or services (even if they are not needed now) and to provide appropriate documentation.

Determining the amount and type of documentation that is reasonable is a medical and legal exercise. The medical professional documenting a neuro psychiatric disability may have to function both as a scientist and as an advocate. Testing, observation, medical examinations, and interviews support the diagnosis. Where the purpose of the diagnosis is to assist in obtaining services or academic adjustments in school or accommodations in the workplace, the diagnosis must also support the legal finding that the patient is "otherwise qualified" (though this is presumed in public elementary and secondary school) and is an "individual with a disability" as those terms appears in the law.

As a practical matter then, you must "document" your patient's disability by presenting that amount of evidence necessary to persuade the individuals with whom you are dealing or, in the event that more formal proceedings become necessary, by proving entitlement by a preponderance of the evidence. That is legal language which means essentially that your evidence must be more convincing than that of your opponent. Since you can never know for certain when you will be called on to support your client's case with testimony, your documentation should be developed with care.

Confidentiality Concerns

Confidentiality may be a major concern for individuals with disabilities. There are several sources of requirements which define when and on what terms confidential information must be protected.

Generally, information is public unless its dissemination is prohibited by: 1) a contract, 2) a constitutional law, 3) statutory provisions and their implementing regulations, or 4) court decisions. Of these, two that are important for the pediatric psychiatrists are contractual agreements (with patients, health care providers, insurance companies, etc.) and state law statutory provisions applicable to the practice of psychiatry in the particular state. Arrangements with patients and their families as to confidentiality should be clear and, of course, should be adhered to in a professional manner.

States have laws which require confidentiality for information furnished to certain professionals. These laws carry with them criminal penalties for unauthorized disclosure. Violations by professionals of these laws may also be punished by suspension or revocation of professional licenses. Each state has its own definition of the classes of professionals whose patient/client communications are considered privileged. Virtually all states recognize as confidential communications made to clergymen, medical doctors and lawyers. Psychologists are frequently also included. However, professionals who are not listed in the statutes of a particular state, but who perform functions similar to those of listed professionals, may not be covered. Thus, in *Thompson v. State,* [32] the court held that communications made to a "crisis intervention specialist" were not protected under a statute creating a psychotherapist/patient privilege.

The psychotherapist/patient privilege is not absolute. Cases have upheld the duty of a psychiatrist where the patient is a danger to another to use reasonable care to protect an intended victim. The privilege did not block enforcement of subpoenas issued to psychiatrists during an insurance fraud investigation. The requested information pertained to patient identities and treatment lengths. [33]

The United States Supreme Court recognized the applicability of the therapist/patient privilege in *Jaffee ex rel. Allen v. Redmond, et al.* [34] In that case, an on-duty police officer (Redmond) employed by a village as a security guard killed Allen in the line of duty. Allen's estate sued Redmond for violations of federal civil rights laws. The court ordered Redmond to give the plaintiff notes made by Karen Beyer, a licensed clinical social worker, during counseling sessions with Redmond after the shooting, rejecting their argument that a psychotherapist's patient privilege protected the contents of the conversations. The trial court found that they were not protected.

The Supreme Court held that the conversations between Redmond and her therapist and the notes taken during their counseling sessions are protected from compelled disclosure under the Federal Rules of Evidence (FRE) which govern all trials in federal court. The High Court ruled that FRE 501 authorizes federal courts to define new privileges by interpreting "the principles of the common law . . . in the light of reason and experience." Rule 501, the Supreme Court held, directed the federal courts to "continue the evolutionary development of testimonial privileges."

The court held that the federal privilege applies to psychiatrists and psychologists, but ruled that it also extends to confidential communications made to licensed social workers in the course of psychotherapy. The reasons for recognizing the privilege for treatment by psychiatrists and psychologists, in the Supreme Court's view, apply with equal force to clinical social workers, which the court noted, have been recognized by the vast majority of States. The court said the following:

> *Significant private interests support recognition of a psychotherapist privilege. Effective psychotherapy depends upon an atmosphere of confidence and trust, and therefore the mere possibility of disclosure of confidential communications may impede development of the relationship necessary for successful treatment. The privilege also serves the public interest, since the mental health of the Nation's citizenry, no less than its physical health, is a public good of transcendent importance.*

The court cautioned that "Because this is the first case in which this Court has recognized a psychotherapist privilege, it is neither necessary nor feasible to delineate its full contours in a way that would govern all future questions."

But the Supreme Court's ruling does suggest an underlying set of principles which it intends to follow. Specifically, the court intends to recognize as a matter of federal law that communications between a provider of mental health services and a "client" will be treated as privileged. It also indicated that a "provider of mental health services" includes anyone authorized by state law to elicit information from people with the expectation of privacy for the purpose of counseling or treating them.

It is important to note that, in this case, it was the plaintiff who sought the therapist's records concerning the defendant. The defendant's mental condition was only marginally relevant to the plaintiff's case.

However, in an ADA/RA case, the claimant's mental make-up is the central issue, because the trial court must decide whether the claimant has a mental or physical impairment which substantially limits a major life activity and whether or not she/he is "qualified". The court did not address the question of whether the plaintiff's therapist in such a case can lawfully be required to disclose the contents of therapy sessions which might support the defendant's contentions that the plaintiff was not qualified to enroll in a particular academic program or to be hired for a particular job.

Federal laws provide confidentiality protections for children and adults with disabilities. The IDEA provides for confidentiality of school records concerning students with disabilities.[35] Regulations provide that these records may be retained permanently by the school unless the parents request that the records be destroyed. The only records that need not be destroyed following such a request are the student's name, address, and phone number, grades, attendance record, grade level completed, and year completed.[36]

At the college level, the IDEA does not apply, but protections are provided by the Family Educational Rights and Privacy Act (FERPA), which was passed in 1974 and is also known as the Buckley Amendment. It affords students the right to have access to their educational records, requires their consent to release of records to third parties, and allows students to challenge information in their records. FERPA applies to all colleges that receive federal funds.

Statutes and regulations establish rules of general applicability. On a showing of necessity, courts may authorize or prohibit the release of records based on the factual necessities of the case.

Summary

To qualify for entitlements and to assert the rights of individuals with disabilities, one must meet the appropriate legal standard. These standards vary depending on the particular statute involved. Under the RA and ADA, an individual with an impairment that substantially limits a major life activity is entitled to reasonable accommodation in education, professional licensing and employment.

These laws are not self-executing. To obtain their benefits, you must show that his/her impairments are of sufficient severity to constitute disabilities under the applicable standard and that the particular entitlement, service, or accommodation is appropriate.

Notes

1   New York v. Mid Hudson Medical Group, No. 94 Civ. 4688 (HB) (S.D.N.Y. 1995).

2   Delmonte v. Florida Dep't of Business & Professional Regulation, 877 F. Supp. 1563 (S. D. Fla. 1995).

3   29 U.S.C.A. § 706 (8)(b)(i)(1995); See also 42 U.S.C.A. § 12102(2); Fitzgerald v. Green Valley Area Educ. Agency, 589 F. Supp. 1130 (S.D. Iowa 1984).

4   29 CFR § 1613.702(b)(2).

5   The Rehabilitation Act of 1973, 29 U.S.C.A. § 701 et seq.(1995); Civil Service Reform Act of 1978, 5 U.S.C.A. § 2302 et seq. (1995).

6   The Americans with Disabilities Act of 1990, 42 U.S.C.A. § 12209 (1995).

7   29 U.S.C.A. § 794 et seq. (1995). This section is often informally referred to as "Section 504", its designation in the Public Law which Congress originally enacted.

8   29 U.S.C.A. § 793 et seq. (1995).

9   Stutts v. Freeman , 694 F. 2d 666 (11th Cir. 1983).

10 United States v. Becker C. P. A. Review, 1993 WL 632257 (D.D.C. 1993).

11 Lynch v. Department of Educ., 52 M.S.P.R. 541 (1992); but see Bolstein v. Reich, 1995 WL 46387 (D.D.C.), aff'd, 1995 WL 686236 (D.C. Cir. 1995), DOL attorney with depression which prevented him from performing independent, unsupervised high level legal analysis, research and writing is not otherwise qualified where these skills are essential features of his job.

12 United States Equal Employment Opportunity Commission: The Americans with Disability Act: Your Rights as an Individual EEOC-BK-18 (1991).

13 20 U. S. C. A. § 1400 et seq.(1995).

14 See, for example, 34 C.F.R. §§ 104.33, 10435 and 10436 (1995).

15 United States v. Becker C. P. A. Review, 1993 WL 632257 (D.D.C. 1993).

16 28 C.F.R. § 36.309(b)(1)(i) (1995).

17 28 C.F.R. § 36.309(b)(2) (1995).

18 Letter from W. Smith, Acting Assistant Secretary for Civil Rights, U.S. Department of Education, to Neill Stern, Executive Vice President, Parker College of Chiropractic , March 6, 1990, at 3-4.

19 28 C.F.R. § 36.309 et seq. (1995)

20 United States v. Becker C. P. A. Review, 1993 WL 632257 (D.D.C. 1993).

21 Wynne v. Tufts University School of Medicine, 932 F.2d 19 (1st Cir. 1991).

22 Weintraub v. Board of Bar Examiners, SJC. No. OE-0087 (Mass. 1992).

23 United States v. Board of Trustees for the University of Alabama, 908 F.2d 740 (11th Cir. 1990).

24 University of Arizona, Letter of Findings (LOF) OCR Docket No. 09-91-2402; 2 NDLR¶ 285.

25 Halasz v. University of New England, 816 F. Supp. 37 (D. Me. 1993).

26 Pazer v. New York State Board of Law Examiners, 849 F. Supp. 284 (S.D.N.Y. 1994).

27 849 F. Supp. 284 at 287.

28 29 C.F.R. § 1630.2(i)(1995).

29 Fitzgerald v. Green Valley Area Educ. Agency, 589 F. Supp. 1130 (S.D. Iowa 1984).

30 28 C.F.R. § 36.201(a) (1995).

31 Pandazides v. Virginia Bd. of Educ., 804 F. Supp. 794, 803 (E.D. Va. 1992); reversed on other grounds, 13 F.3d 823.

32 Thompson v. State, 615 So. 2d 737 (Fla. Dist. Ct. App. 1993).

33 In re Zuniga, 714 F.2d 632 (6th Cir., cert. denied, 464 U.S. 983 (1983).

34 Jaffee ex rel. Allen v. Redmond, et al. Docket 95-266 — Decided June 13, 1996; the Supreme Court.

35 20 U.S.C. A. § 1417(c) (1995).

36 34 C.F.R. § 300.573 (1995).

Chapter Six

Keys to Success in College for Students with Learning Disabilities: Self-Knowledge, Self-Advocacy, and Individualized Support Services

Maureen K. Riley, M.Ed.

Maureen K. Riley, M. Ed., is professor of special education and psychology and director of Academic Support Services for students with learning disabilities at Leslsey College in Cambridge, Massachusetts. Ms. Riley serves as vice president of the board of directors of the Learning Disabilities Association of Massachusetts.

Something we were withholding made us weak
Until we found it was ourselves
We were withholding from our land of living
And forthwith found salvation in surrender.
Such as we were we gave ourselves outright...
Robert Frost

Overview

For students with learning disabilities, success at the postsecondary level is first and foremost fostered by the students' appreciation of themselves, of their personal and intellectual strengths, and of the academic achievement which earned them acceptance to college. This self-understanding is the necessary foundation for the essential skill of self-advocacy. In the best of circumstances, the students' self-understanding and self-advocacy skills are sustained by involvement with an informed and committed learning disability support program.

Self-Understanding and Misunderstandings

When students with self-identified learning disabilities are accepted at a college or university, they have been objectively evaluated by the admissions committee to fulfill the legal category "otherwise qualified" (ADA, 1990). That is, they have been judged to possess the intellectual abilities and the necessary academic preparation to meet the essential requirements of that college. By very definition, and confirmed by diagnostic testing, students characterized as LD are of average or above average intelligence. It is noteworthy that, after decades of evidence which substantiates the intellectual strengths of students with learning disabilities and which documents their neurologically-based information processing needs, misunderstandings about the definition persist.

It happens in some institutions of higher education that controversies materialize. Ironically, questions arise challenging both the capabilities of students with learning disabilities to do college work and the students' need for accommodations (Guckenberger v. Boston University, 1997; Nealon, 1997; Roberts and Mather, 1995). Students themselves, therefore, benefit from a well-grounded understanding of their own strengths and needs.

Different Ways of Knowing and Expressing

More appropriately, the term LD should stand for "learning difference;" students accepted to college have obviously proven that they are well able to learn. Some special educators fear, however, that using the term, "learning difference," could contribute to a lack of appreciation of the serious struggles that can exist for a student functioning with a learning disability. It is critical that students with LD are provided the opportunity to learn and to express themselves in the varied ways essential to their achievement. The dilemma arises when these ways do not fit traditional educational practices; concerns are raised, then, about the maintenance of academic standards.

The legitimacy of students with learning disabilities to meet academic standards in alternative modes of assessment has been demonstrated in research. Studies have shown that grade school students with learning disabilities can fail or succeed in expressing what they know directly in relation to the design of the test format. Students were able to express their knowledge of challenging science content when it was presented in an alternative format. The students with learning disabilities were significantly less successful with content presented in the traditional verbal, multiple choice test format. With equally challenging content questions, presented on the same science concepts in a visual-graphic multiple choice format, the students ably demonstrated their knowledge of the subject matter. This was true also for the content in other alternative assessment modes: constructed diagram and drawing. (see Appendix A pg. 80) (Dalton, Tivnan, Riley, Rawson, & Dias, 1995; Riley, 1996).

For college students with learning disabilities, variations in performance are evidenced on modified exam formats. Many students with learning disabilities consistently lose credit in particular sections of exams. For example, many lose credit on sections with multiple choice questions, and in contrast, can be successful with the same content in essay form. For some students, the opposite pattern is true. When different modes of expression are required within the same question in an exam, this contrast in performance can occur. The student can be successful with the solution to a complex math or science problem, but notably lose credit when written explanations of the process are required about the very same problem. Many of these students, however, are able to provide a correct verbal explanation of the process, orally (Riley, 1991). For students with learning disabilities, it is critical that they continually evaluate their effectiveness in relation to the varied contexts in which they are required to perform. They need to grow in this self-understanding in order to select appropriate accommodations which allow them to express what they know. The central issue is that academic standards must be honored and can be rigorously met by alternative modes of assessment and expression.

Stories to Tell

Students with learning disabilities almost universally have stories to tell of difficult times in their lives in which they have felt frustrated to appear less capable than they are. These situations occur out of school as well as in school and often involve the processing of certain kinds of basic information needed quickly or "on demand." Typical examples include being called upon to remember the short cut to compute the tip for a bill in a restaurant or to come up with a well-known fact or famous name upon demand in a classroom. In spite of being told that they are intelligent, these everyday experiences are unsettling and can undermine confidence. In the new environment of higher education, old doubts can resurface.

When I don't do well on something, I have the feeling I'm going to be "discovered," that they'll find out that I'm really not as smart as they thought when they accepted me.

Building Upon Intellectual Strengths

Identifying specific strengths and needs is not a simple process. Students come to see that they may have both strengths and difficulties even within the same academic area. Students may struggle with expository writing and yet express themselves powerfully through the medium of poetry.

In a large crowded auditorium with a stage and an amphitheater with ascending rows of seats, Naomi and Suzanne sat about two thirds of the way up. Both had received the prestigious distinction of having their poems accepted to the college Humanities literary publication. Both were students with learning disabilities with very different academic backgrounds. One had attended private, special education schools and the other urban public schools. Together they had decided that they would not be going down on stage to read their poetry; they would just listen to the others. Each, at different times during the readings, did eventually make the move to walk down the steep aisle steps and up onto the stage to read. They both knew it was a legitimate moment for them; their work was placed among the writings of some of the finest students in the college.

The venue of poetry bypassed the difficulties both these students had with syntax when writing. Their intellectual strengths, their high conceptual ability and gifts with imagery, were manifest when they were not constrained by their problems with syntax. Importantly, their success in an area of strength became a source of strong motivation and energy to work on their expository writing. Addressing difficulties with complex syntax was a time-consuming process fraught with the frustration of revisions upon revisions (Wiig & Semel, 1984). Over time with tutorial support, they came to see that it was something that could be mastered.

Political and Legal Factors

In addition to a clear perspective on their own issues, students entering college need to appreciate that broader political and legal issues, which may seem remote to them, will impact their academic lives. The college community reflects the larger educational community in the progress – and the lack of progress – in understanding how to implement the laws in the real world of the general education classroom. The transformation, inevitably, will take time and will involve stages of both understanding and misunderstanding. Students with learning disabilities need to know the history of this evolution in order to anticipate the diverse mindsets and possible misconceptions they may encounter. If they are informed, they will be better able to negotiate and self-advocate with administrators and faculty to arrange academic accommodations.

Inclusion in Higher Education

Due to federal legislation, the number of students with learning disabilities at postsecondary institutions has continued to increase throughout the 1980's and 1990's (Adelman & Wren, 1990; Mangrum & Strichart, 1988). Faculty and staff now are faced with accommodating the increased diversity in the student body. The increased diversity is due both to changes in demographics bringing students with English as a second language, as well the influx of students with diverse special needs. The field of special education has been developing and applying instructional techniques and curricula over the years, yet extending these practices into the general education setting has proven not to be a simple process (Baker & Zigmond, 1990; Fuchs, Roberts, Fuchs, Bowers, 1996). Higher education is experiencing some of the same frustrations and difficulties described by teachers throughout the K-12 system (Lenz et al., 1995).

Prior to this change, the fundamental model for teaching and learning in institutions of higher education had remained relatively unchanged throughout the century. Except for a small number of colleges with innovative programming, the dominant college instructional model consisted of a lecture-notetaking-timed-exams format, with small group seminar as one of the few variations in the model. Prior to federal legislation which required that accommodations be made, individuals with learning disabilities who participated within this well-established model included only that small percentage who were able to cope without accommodations (ADA, 1990; IDEA, 1990).

While support programs were being developed throughout the 1980's, studies reporting on faculty attitude reveal that this was not an easy adjustment for those teaching in higher education. A significant percentage of faculty expressed that, given the option, they would choose not to admit students with learning disabilities. They also doubted the ability of students with learning disabilities attending their institutions to complete their degrees (Aksamit, Morris, & Leuenberger, 1987; Leyser, 1989; Minner and Prater, 1984). This mindset should not come as a shock, however, since the majority of college faculty had never been trained in, or been responsible for developing special needs instructional approaches, throughout their professional lives. Full inclusion came suddenly to postsecondary education. Unlike the K-12 educational system, special education programming had not been an integral part of higher education.

In the 1990's, there are many more institutions with support programs for students with learning disabilities in higher education, but even where there are the best of intentions, there is still much to be learned about program development at the postsecondary level (Patton & Polloway, 1996). As well as the efforts made by the student and the support specialist, collaboration with administrators, faculty, and staff is required in order to effect program and course adjustments. At the level of implementation of accommodations, there continues to be a lack of understanding, as well as misunderstanding regarding the interpretation of the legislation (Martin, 1992b). Even with the protection of the laws, there are still students who are not receiving curricular accommodations (Roberts & Mather, 1995).

The Right to Accommodations

In spite of the magnitude of the challenge, major federal legislation has solidly established the rights of persons with learning disabilities to be fully included in institutions of higher education (ADA, 1990; IDEA, 1990; Riley, 1998). Upon acceptance, the college has committed to provide "reasonable accommodations" within the academic program to address the specific, documented needs of the student. As part of their self-advocacy repertoire, students need to know their rights; they need to understand unequivocally that, in seeking accommodations, they are not asking for privileges or unrealistic support.

I don't want any favors. I want to fulfill my responsibilities so that I know I really earned my degree.

If they are designed appropriately, accommodations only "level the playing field" and do not provide unfair advantage (Alster, 1997; Riley, 1998; Runyan, 1991). There must be a match between the specific, documented needs of the student and the accommodation. The law explicitly requires that the accommodations do not lower academic standards or cause the institution to forego essential requirements.

Accommodations in Higher Education

Significant differences in achievement can be attained with the appropriate accommodations. With a thoughtful, deliberate process in place, accommodations are practical and workable for both student and faculty (see Appendix B pg. 81) (Riley, 1998). Once the eligibility is determined, some accommodations, such as the commonly applied extended time for exams, can be established as a simple routine for a student throughout the course. However, even this basic accommodation does involve keeping a record of the established accommodation, giving a form of notification to the professor, planning of available space, and the dispatching of the exam. The process can be facilitated for the student and the professor by appropriate forms and a predictable system.

Some students with specific reading difficulties may require readers for exams. Directions and questions for examinations typically involve heavily embedded language.

> *I hate myself for how I lost the points on the exam. The professor wrote that it was an intelligent essay, but that it didn't answer the question asked.*

In order to prevent this, the reader rereads the question for the student until she or he evidences understanding of the question. Procedures need to be established and training provided for the reader. To ensure academic standards, the reader does not discuss the topic or offer interpretation of the question.

The Need for Individualization

It can be disconcerting to those without training in the field of special education to realize that students with learning disabilities do not necessarily share the same, predictable set of characteristics. Adults with learning disabilities embody a heterogeneous group of individuals resulting in discrete responses to varied contexts and content. Yet, "the precise nature of students' academic difficulties" is considered "essential" for developing support programs for college students with LD (Hughes & Smith, 1990, p. 76). It has been confirmed across a number of research studies on inclusion that individualization of instruction has been identified as a necessary condition for successful inclusion of students with learning disabilities (Lenz et al., 1995). Individualization has been identified as a demanding goal to achieve because there are no generic accommodations; one "suit" just won't fit all (Morocco, Riley, Gordon & Howard, 1996; Riley, Morocco, Gordon & Howard, 1993).

Conventional Practices from a Different Perspective

The design of routine accommodations can require an inventive perspective in order to honor the academic standards of the professor and to the meet the individual needs of the student. A math professor, for example, challenged the preservation of academic standards when having to provide a reader for the math exam. It was his best judgment that simple, unintentional emphasis by the reader on specific words in a problem could provide cues to the student. The professor, the student and the learning disability specialist met to work out an option. The professor generously offered to tape record the exam problems himself, and in that sense, become the reader for the student. To the student, surprisingly, the option of taped questions sounded like a nightmare.

The student explained that there would be ten problems, all with parts, and that he liked to do the problems out of order in order to work on the problems he knew best, first. He learned from past experience with audio tapes that, for him, searching back and forth on the tape among the math problems would be totally disorganizing due to his difficulties with spatial orientation, left, right, etc. The learning disability specialist suggested using ten tapes, one for each problem, all of which afterwards could be simply erased and re-used, avoiding any expense. It was an unconventional, but effective approach to the alternative testing and demonstration of productive collaboration by faculty, staff and student. Academic standards were maintained and the intellectually qualified student was able to be a full and successful participant in the math course. It was an everyday situation simply viewed from a different perspective (Gamble, 1993).

Another novel accommodation involved a student with an attention disorder who consistently and curiously received almost all of the credit on the first half of her exams and then lost almost all the points in the second half. In reviewing her exams, the learning disability specialist inquired how she could write such confused statements in the last half that were in such extreme contrast to the high quality of the answers in earlier sections. As strange as it might appear to those not familiar with attention disorders, she explained that, due to her attention difficulties and hyperactivity, she literally could not stand to sit in the room another minute. She had to get up and leave. She just wrote anything because she couldn't think any longer. She was unable to sustain her attention (Barkley, 1997).

The student had been "hiding out" from the professor because she was embarrassed to explain her attention disorder. She was afraid he would think she was "weird." She needed support for self-understanding regarding the legitimacy of her needs and for self-advocacy to develop a plan for the accommodation. She did make the request and arranged with the professor to take half of the exam; she would then turn it in that half, take a break and come back to do the second half. Her option was to go for a run during the break. The professor insured that academic standards were maintained. She could not add to the first half of the exam when she returned, and she had not seen the second half so that, on break, it was not possible for her to seek outside sources. Her test grades improved dramatically. These unusual accommodations are not expensive or difficult to arrange, but can make vital differences in students' lives. In order to self-advocate for appropriate accommodations in college, students need to be thinking about how uniquely their difficulties can play themselves out in the different content areas and with the varied kinds of requirements.

Sources of Misunderstandings

One source of the lack of understanding is that, typically, learning disabilities and attention disorders are invisible disabilities. The factors creating the obstacles to learning are not as apparent as the limitations of disabilities which have physically evident characteristics. This makes the disability less comprehensible and, somehow, to be interpreted as less significant or, even, as not real. Daily, simple misunderstandings also occur.

> *Janice, a first year student, went into the registrar's office to pick up a form for a course change. Janice began to leave, but was called back and asked if she would fill the form out right away. Janice offered that she would bring it back shortly. She was told that time was a factor to get the change into the computer. Janice turned and walked out of the office. To the registrar, Janice appeared to be a rude and difficult person.*

What Janice didn't feel comfortable explaining was that she has problems with spelling and inordinate difficulty with her fine motor ability. She needed both a spell checker and considerable time to be able to write small enough to fit her handwriting inside the fine lines and blocks on the form.

I just couldn't stand looking so stupid.

With training in metacognition, Janice gained the conviction that the lower order abilities of fine motor and spelling skills are not indicators of intelligence. In self-advocacy training, she role played ways to handle the issue. She learned to address these irritating, but trivial difficulties in a straightforward and knowledgeable manner. She built the confidence to cope with such situations in the future.

Conflicting Expectations

The misconceptions about learning disabilities can run the gamut from low expectations, such as questioning the students' ability to perform college level work at a high level to impractical, elevated expectations, such as questioning why the students cannot meet requirements with greater ease and efficiency. Students too often conclude that these misunderstandings arise out of some lack in themselves, rather than from a lack of understanding on the part of others.

Those who are able to perform the subskills underlying academic tasks with relative ease can find it extremely difficult to understand that an intelligent person can become bewildered and fatigued by the repetitive demand of the more elementary tasks underlying academic requirements. They need to be informed, as the students themselves need to internalize, that the efforts of persons with learning disabilities, paradoxically, are more typically thwarted by lower levels of information processing, such as spelling and the decoding of text, than by the rigorous conceptual demands involved. An expression used in the field which has validity states that students with learning disabilities find simple tasks difficult and difficult tasks easier.

Decoding versus Comprehension

Jon needs to read and reread his texts. He told his professors that he was having great difficulty comprehending the readings for his courses. With this wording, he misrepresented himself; he made it sound as if he was not capable of comprehending the content of his courses. It was not unreasonable, therefore, for his professors to question whether he was capable of participating in the program. His diagnostic testing actually identified him as a gifted student with learning disabilities. The constraint was Jon's laborious, time consuming process of decoding the text.

When he would get beyond "the ink on the page" and move to the level of meaning, he was highly capable of comprehending the content. He lacked the metacognitive understanding of these distinctions in his abilities that he needed to self-advocate appropriately. As well as providing the metacognitive perspective on his reading, the learning disability specialist provided information about the federally supported Taped Books from Recordings for the Blind and Dyslexic (see Appendix C pg. 84). The taped text books proved a highly effective accommodation for him.

Basically, I'd just read it, and it wouldn't click at all. I don't want to get emotional, but it's really almost like a rebirth. I get kind of upset because all my life it's been like that. Now, I sit down and I have the book and the tape, and I follow along, speed it up, turn it over. I was watching a TV commercial with an older man talking about how he just learned to read, and it feels like that.

Perceptual versus Conceptual

Ironically, a more subtle but common misinterpretation takes place when the intellectual strengths of a student with learning disabilities are evidenced in a rigorous assignment. The reasoning projected by the instructor is that the ability to perform in that context predicts performance of the student in future assignments. The student's failure to live up to that assumption in another assignment with different demands can lead to the interpretation that it is the student's lack of motivation or preparation that is operating. Accommodations may be not be needed in one situation, and yet they may be essential under apparently similar conditions. Two tasks may appear to be of equivalent demand, but due to the intricacies of a learning disability, subtle, silent factors can confound a task.

A student with an "A" average in math quizzes throughout a course tried to explain to her professor that her confusion on the geometry problems in the final exam was due to the lined pages in the exam "blue book."

I got disoriented. I couldn't keep things lined up. I kept erasing and reworking the problems.

It could sound like a bizarre excuse, but many students with learning disabilities have visual perceptual difficulties. In this situation, the lines on the page created visual figure ground factors and hindered her ability to solve the problems.

Language Reception and Expression

It sounds unbelievable but during my admissions interview, I actually misinterpreted what the admissions person said about my acceptance. What I heard her say was that I was not accepted. But, in actuality, what she said was she needed my grades and transcript from my other college and a letter from my high school explaining their grading system since they don't do letter grades.

Katie has particular difficulty with syntax when listening to language; she often hears mostly contentives, that is, the individual words with referential meaning, and she can lose the functional words which are the connectives. When she was more at ease, Katie would ordinarily ask for repeats in discussion. What Katie heard during the interview were the contentives – "transcript," "grades" – which carried an intimidating association for her. For her, the general tone of the message was that better grades were needed to be accepted. She walked out of the office believing she had been rejected. Fortunately, the counselor eventually called her to simply ask her why she hadn't sent the additional information requested.

Katie was later able to laugh at that experience and used it as incentive for developing accommodations. One of the accommodations she used regularly was audio taping her classes, both lecture and discussion. She replayed the tapes as she traveled the one and a half hour trip on a bus to and from the college, four days a week. She interrupted the tape to take notes.

She proved her ability to herself and to her instructors in challenging courses, in particular with her philosophy and political science papers. She expressed herself well in writing papers, she explained, because she could take the time to formulate the wording of her ideas. For exams, she used the accommodation of extended time. In class, she could also concentrate exclusively on listening to the ideas because taping allowed her to develop her notes at a later time. For class participation, Katie self-advocated and spoke with her professors to explain that it took her a little longer to formulate a complex answer spontaneously. She requested that she be able to adopt the technique of responding to the professor's question with the statement, "Can you come back to me in a minute with that question?" With this accommodation, she didn't sit through class anymore in fear of being called on.

Success in Higher Education

Students with learning disabilities can benefit from listening to stories of the ways in which their peers are devising accommodations to achieve in college. Knowing that reasonable accommodations which honor academic standards are available and workable can deflect unnecessary frustration or discouragement (see Appendix B pg. 81). Students with learning disabilities are succeeding and graduating from college (Vogel & Adelman, 1992). Anticipating challenges and envisioning possible solutions can facilitate success.

I don't spend my energy worrying anymore. I know I can do it. Doing the work still takes me a longer time than other people, but I know it's doable.

Most of my accommodations are all set. I know now what I need. Only once in a while I run into a snag, but I don't panic about it. I'm doing really well academically. I feel good about myself and my work. I'm actually happier than I've ever been in school, happier than I ever thought I would be.

APPENDIX A
ALTERNATIVE TEST FORMATS1

Type of Assessment	Primary Symbol System	Openness of Response	Example (series circuit)
Multiple Choice	Visual	Closed	Which diagram shows what happens when a bulb burns out in a series circuit?
	Verbal	Closed	Ernesto wired a white bulb and a blue bulb in a series circuit. What do you think happened when the white bulb burned out? a. both bulbs lit b. only the blue bulb lit c. only the shite bulb lit d. neither bulb lit
Constructed Diagram	Visual/ Verbal	Constrained	 Will bulb #3 light? no If yes, draw the pathway in red. If no, what's the problem? because the other bulb is burned out Will bulb #4 light? no If yes, draw the pathway in red. If no, what's the problem? because it is burned out
Questionnaire	Visual/ Verbal	Open	Sue had a string of tree lights. She unscrewed 1 bulb and the all the bulbs went out. Why? The sircut broke Draw a large diagram to show how the bulbs could be wired in the circuit.
Hands-on Performance	Manipulative	Open	(Note in previous challenge students were asked to make the bulb in a simple circuit burn brighter). Now add a bulb so that if one of these bulbs goes out, the other bulb will also go out. Again, tell me what you are thinking as you're working so I can understand better. (When student is finsihed, ask: • What happens to make both bulbs light up? • (Point to bulb nearest battery) What would happen if this bulb burned out? • Would the other bulb still light? If no, why not? If yes, have student test it out and ask, So the other bulb didn't light, why not?

APPENDIX B
ACCOMMODATIONS

TESTING ACCOMMODATIONS

Setting Altered
- Administer the test in a separate location, individually.
- Administer the test in a location with minimal distractions.
- Administer the test in a study carrel, individually.
- Provide special lighting.
- Administer the test to a small group in a separate location.

Time and/or Schedule Changes
- Extend the time allotted to complete the test.
- Allow frequent breaks during testing.
- Consider the time of the day that is best for the student.
- Administer the test in several sessions.
- Administer the test over several days.
- Consider a flexible schedule/at different day or week.

Changes in Test Format
- Increase spacing between items and lines, or reduce items per page or line.
- Highlight key words or phrases in directions.
- Limit reading passages with one complete sentence per line.
- Allow the student to mark responses in the booklet rather than on bubble answer sheet.
- Increase the size of answer sheet bubbles.
- Employ a reader for directions, with clarification.
- Employ a reader for questions (as appropriate, with or without clarification).
- Request audiotape of test.
- Request the test on computer/use of word processor (as appropriate, with or without spell check).
- Have the computer read to the student.
- Give dictation to a proctor/scribe.
- Use a calculator.
- Use a place marker.

APPENDIX B
ACCOMMODATIONS
(continued)

INSTRUCTIONAL ACCOMMODATIONS

- taped textbooks/readings;
- readers;
- note-taking modifications:
  note takers/paid or volunteer list or class member volunteer;
  class member volunteer uses two-copy carbonless paper (plain or graphed for math/science) or notes photocopied by student with LD;
  tape recorder;
  laptop computer;

- syllabus and course requirement handouts several weeks in advance;
- formative evaluation/feedback prior to final products on assignments;
- alternative assignment/equivalent level of challenge;
- extended time on assignments;
- extra credit assignments;
- no penalty for spelling/grammar errors in spontaneous writing, such as for exams, in-class
- writing or use of portable spell check (except where literacy is requisite);
- tutoring for course content/subject matter/course assignments; and
- auxiliary aids (personal/library/computer center) (See Appendix C.)

PROGRAM ACCOMMODATIONS

- Interview and review of diagnostic testing with LD service provider (if self-identified).
- Request special housing (e.g., single room or dorm with quiet study areas).
- Seek priority registration.
- Seek full-time status with minimal reduction in courseload (financial aid considerations).

APPENDIX B
ACCOMMODATIONS
(continued)

- Seek part-time program/with full-time services, extra-curricular and dorm privileges.
- Audit courses (no fee) to be taken in another semester or as prep for a different course.
- Consider independent study course for challenge area.
- Take reviews/remedial courses for non-credit or credit (e.g., math, writing).
- Use the LD Academic Support Services Center.
- Consult the LD Specialist Service Provider/Advocate/Advisor.

APPENDIX C

TECHNOLOGICAL AIDS

*Portable Spell-Checker/Dictionary/Thesaurus/Speech: Pronounces Target Word
English/Other Languages*
      Franklin Learning Resources
      122 Burrs Road
      Mt. Holly, NJ 08060
      800-525-9673

Talking Calculator
      Sharp Talking Calculator EL-640
      Sharp Electronics Corporation
      Sharp Plaza
      20600 South Alameda Street
      Carson, CA 90810
      213-637-9488

*Speech
Note*:

      Apple Macintosh computers with System 7 or later are capable of
      Text to Speech.

      IBM and compatibles with Windows 95 are capable of Text to
      Speech, but require an added sound card.

      textHELP
      HumanWare, Inc.
      6245 King Road
      Loomis, CA 95650
      916-652-7253

      Kurzweil 3000
      Kurzweil Personal Reader
      HumanWare, Inc.
      6245 King Road
      Loomis, CA 95650
      916-652-7253

Scanner
>Epson America, Inc.
>20770 Madrona Ave.
>Mail Stop C2-02
>Torrance, CA 90509-2843
>310-782-2600
>800-463-7766
>
>Hewlett Packard Company
>3000 Hanover St.
>Palo Alto, CA 94304-1185
>650-857-1501
>
>Microtek Lab, Inc.
>3715 Doolittle Dr.
>Redondo Beach, CA 90278-1226
>310-297-5000
>800-654-4160

Recorded Texts
>**Computerized Books**
>Computerized Books for the Blind
>37 Corbin Hall
>University of Montana
>Missoula, MT 59812
>406-243-5481
>
>**Recorded Books**
>Library of Congress
>National Library Service for the Blind and Physically Handicapped
>1291 Taylor St., NW
>Washington, DC 20542
>202-707-5100
>
>**Recorded Books**
>Recording for the Blind, Inc.
>20 Roszel Road
>Princeton, NJ 08540
>609-452-0606
>http://www.rfbd.org

Four-track Tape Recorders / Variable Speech Control
>Handi-Cassette
>American Printing House for the Blind, Inc.
>1839 Frankfort Avenue
>P.O. Box 6085
>Louisville, KY
>502-895-2405

>Recording for the Blind, Inc.
>20 Roszel Road
>Princeton, NJ 08540
>609-452-0606
>800-221-4792
>http://www.rfbd.org

>GE Fastrac
>General Electric
>P.O. Box 1976
>Indianapolis, IN 46206
>800-447-1700

Speech to Text
>Dragon Dictate
>Dragon Systems, Inc.
>320 Nevada Street
>Newton, MA 02160
>617-965-5200

>VoiceType Simply Speaking
>IBM
>Old Orchard Road
>Armonk, NY 10504

Graphic Organizing Software: Generate and Organize Ideas through Mapping,
Webbing, Outlining
>Inspiration
>Inspiration Software, Inc.
>2920 SW Dolph Court, Suite 3
>Portland, OR 97219
>503-245-9011

Proofreading Software
      Grammatik IV
      Reference Software
      330 Townsend Street, Suite 123
      San Francisco, CA 94107
      415-541-0222

      Correct Grammar
      Writing Tools Group
      1 Harbor Drive, Suite 111
      Sausalito, CA 94965
      415-332-8692

Personal Data Manager: Software
      WordPerfect Library
      WordPerfect Corporation
      1555 N. Technology Way
      Orem, UT 84507
      801-225-5000

Personal Data Manager: "Stand Alone"
      Texas Instruments Pocket Solutions Data Banks
      Texas Instruments
      P.O. Box 2500
      Lubbox, TX 79408
      806-747-1882

Mouse Interface Software
      MousePerfect
      MousePerfect, Inc.
      P.O. Box 367
      Clarston, GA 30021

Key Repeat Inhibitor
      Filch
      Kinetic Designs
      14321 Anatevka
      Olalla, WA 98459
      206-857-7943

APPENDIX D

Resource Books on Learning Disabilities
Focusing on Adulthood and College

Adelman, P.B. & Wren, C. T. (1990). *Learning Disabilities, Graduate School, and Careers: The Student's Perspective*. Lake Forest, IL: Barat College.

Brinckerhoff, L.C., Shaw, S. F., & McGuire, J. M. (1993). *Promoting postsecondary education for students with learning disabilities: A handbook for practitioners*. Austin, TX: PRO-ED.

Crocker, J .M. (1992). *Campus opportunities for students with learning disabilities* (2nd ed.). Alexandria, VA: Octameron Associates.

Johnson, D. J. & Blalock, J. W. (1987). *Young adults with learning disabilities: Clinical studies*. Orlando, FL: Grune & Stratton.

Kravets, J. (1993).*The K & W guide to colleges for the learning disabled* (2nd ed.). New York: Harper Collins.

Mangrum, C. T. II, & Strichart, S. S. (Eds.). (1988).*College and the learning disabled student: Program development implementation and selection* (2nd ed.). Orlando, FL: Grune & Stratton.

Mangrum, C. T., & Strichart, S. S. (Eds.). (1988). *Peterson's Guide to Colleges with Programs for Learning-disabled Students* (2nd ed.). Princeton, NJ: Peterson's Guides.

McGuire-Shaw postsecondary selection guide for learning disabled college students. Storrs, CT: University of Connecticut.

Patton, J. R., & Polloway, E. A. (1996). *Learning disabilities: The challenges of adulthood*. Austin, TX: PRO-ED.

Tinto, V. (1987). *Leaving college: Rethinking the causes and cures of student attrition*. Chicago: University of Chicago Press.

Vogel, S. A. & Adelman, P. B. (1993). *Success for college students with learning disabilities: Factors related to educational attainments*. New York: Springer-Verlag.

Vogel, S. A. (1990). *The college student with a learning disability: A handbook for college LD students, admissions officers, faculty and administrators*

Chapter Seven

Students with Learning Disabilities in Graduate School: Access and Accommodation Considerations

Loring C. Brinckerhoff, Ph.D.

Loring Brinckerhoff, Ph.D., is a professor at Tufts University and a consultant on higher education and disability for Recording for the Blind and Dyslexic.

According to recent figures, close to two million students are now enrolled in graduate and professional schools in the United States. In the past 25 years, the number of Americans who have obtained master's degrees has climbed by 60 percent to 350,000 annually (U.S. News & World Report, 1995). Applications to law schools are now gradually dropping from a peak of 94,000 in 1991 to 78,000 applicants in 1995. Columbia University Law School is presently experiencing an eight percent decline in applicants, but none the less, over 6,000 applicants are vying for 340 spots (Johnson, 1995). For the third year in a row, the number of applicants to the nation's 125 medical schools has reached an all-time high. Boston University School of Medicine was deluged with over 12,000 applications for admission for just over 100 openings this year. These figures represent more than twice the number of applicants in 1988.

The composition and demographics of graduate and professional programs are rapidly changing. For example, nearly half of all applicants to medical schools are female, 1 out of 5 applicants represent non-traditional backgrounds, and 8.4 percent of graduate students report a disability (U.S. News & World Report, 1995; Information from HEATH, 1994). These findings indicate that, like their non-disabled counterparts, students with disabilities are knocking on the doors of graduate and professional programs in increasing numbers. In some cases they have been met with skepticism; in other instances they are welcomed. The Association of Academic Psychiatrists (AAP) stated that "medical schools should educate a diverse group of medical students recognizing that in such diversity lies excellence. Included in this group are qualified students who have impairments, functional limitations, and/or disabilities."

This upsurge of interest in graduate studies by individuals with learning disabilities (LD) can be attributed, in part, to greater opportunities that many persons with disabilities are experiencing as a result of the passage of the Americans with Disabilities Act (ADA). The ADA clearly articulates that students with learning disabilities have the same rights to instructional and programmatic access as students with physical disabilities. Furthermore, Title II, (Section 202) of the ADA specifically states that, "no qualified individual with a disability shall, by reason of such disability, be excluded from participation in or be denied the benefits of the services, programs, or activities of a public entity..."

Given these protections under the ADA, job discrimination is less likely, thus increasing the value of a graduate school investment. In addition, the ADA extends coverage to private colleges and universities at both the undergraduate and graduate levels and grants new protections not required previously by the Rehabilitation Act of 1973. For example, individuals who associate with or care for a person with a disability cannot be discriminated against on the basis of their association with a disabled individual (Essex-Sorlie, 1994: Kincaid, 1995). A greater awareness of learning disabilities and Attention Deficit Hyperactivity Disorders (ADHD) by faculty and administrators at the postsecondary level and the proliferation of support services on college campuses in general has encouraged these students to continue their education beyond the undergraduate level (Brinckerhoff, Shaw, & McGuire, 1996; Vogel, 1993).

The intent of this chapter is to explore this new graduate level frontier by broadening the reader's understanding of this unique cohort of students by, a) defining learning disabilities, b) highlighting the characteristics of graduate students with learning disabilities and/or ADHD, c) addressing graduate admissions requirements; and d) determining academic supports and accommodations.

Defining Learning Disabilities

Barbara Bateman (1992), one of the most respected leaders in the field of learning disabilities, noted that, even after a quarter of a century of evolution in this field, we still find individuals who believe that learning disabilities do not exist. Unfortunately, there are still individuals directing our universities, graduate schools, medical schools, and corporate training programs who think that a learning disability is just another fancy excuse for getting special attention. Arthur Frakt, dean of Widener University School of Law, is one of the ADA's most vocal critics. He believes that the ADA is too broad, and law schools in particular have become too accommodating. He contends that, "Everyone who is self-referred to a psychologist or counselor comes back with a diagnosis of a learning disability of some kind" (Cleesattle & Seiberg, 1995). At Boston University, Provost and President-elect Jon Westling complained in a speech to the Heritage Foundation, that laws to protect students with learning disabilities were being used "to force colleges and universities to lower academic standards" (Shapiro, 1996).

The National Joint Committee on Learning Disabilities (NJCLD) defines learning disabilities as the following:

*a general term that refers to a heterogeneous group of disorders
manifested by significant difficulties in the acquisition and use*

*of listening, speaking, reading, writing, reasoning, or mathe-
matical abilities. These disorders are intrinsic to the individual,
presumed to be due to central nervous system dysfunction, and
may occur across the life span. Problems with self-regulatory
behaviors, social perception and social interaction may exist
with learning disabilities but do not by themselves constitute a
learning disability. Although learning disabilities may occur
concomitantly with other handicapping conditions (for example,
sensory impairments, emotional disturbance) or with extrinsic
influences, such as cultural differences and/or insufficient or
inappropriate instruction, they are not the result of those conditions or influences* (NJCLD, 1994).

It is important to point out that not all individuals with learning
disabilities are affected in the same way or to the same degree. The
effects of the disability will vary according to the type and severity of the
LD, the individual's understanding and acceptance of his or her learning
disability, his or her ability to compensate for the learning disability, and
the complexity of the learning task at hand. If more postsecondary service providers adhered to the NJCLD definition, we would not be faced
with the rampant over-identification and misidentification of college students that we now face. Don Hammill (1990) has been one of the guiding
forces behind this definition, and he states that, "The NJCLD never
intended to write the perfect definition, only a better one." He adds that,
"the NJCLD definition provides a viable definitional umbrella under
which all of us may find shelter. It may serve us well during the rainy
days ahead."

Therefore, by definition, individuals with learning disabilities are
a heterogeneous group who possess a wide array of strengths and limitations. By the time LD students are ready to attend graduate school,
they typically have learned how to compensate for their limitations and
to capitalize on their abilities. Gerber and Reiff (1991, 1994) have written
extensively about successful adults with learning disabilities. They suggest that adolescents and adults with learning disabilities need to be
taught to "re-frame" their disability in a more positive manner. The LD
is viewed as just one slice of the student's identity. The research findings
of Gerber, Ginsberg and Reiff (1992) found that successful adults with
learning disabilities often have learned to accept that, despite the learning disability, they can still meet their goals. The implication here is that
"if someone doesn't accept that the learning disability is real and that it

is something he or she will always have to confront, moving ahead is impossible" (p. 171). By recognizing, understanding, and accepting their disability, these students will be better prepared to advocate for themselves, both on campus, and, ultimately, in the world of work.

Characteristics of Graduate Students with Learning Disabilities

Given the heterogeneous nature of this population, it is very difficult to characterize graduate students with learning disabilities as conforming to one specific profile. Students with a prior history of learning disabilities who were fortunate to be accepted into graduate or professional programs often have been diagnosed as both learning disabled *and* gifted. Many of these individuals were able to manage an undergraduate education because of their giftedness, meticulous organization, verbal abilities, and work ethic. They often exhibit significant abilities and creative talents despite some fundamental problems with reading, written language and/or mathematical reasoning and problem solving. This group of students is often misunderstood, in part, because their unique abilities have tended to mask their disabilities.

Students who have a prior history of learning disabilities are often ready to self-identify in the admissions process and to seek help before the semester begins. Those individuals with a history of receiving academic accommodations at the undergraduate level often find it easier to access the same accommodations (e.g., additional time, quiet room, oral exams) since they have a history of success in receiving accommodations. Shaywitz and Shaw (1998) note that gifted/learning disabled students with the highest probability of success at a competitive institution are those who have "had an opportunity to live with the diagnosis and become comfortable, as indicated by the ability to talk openly about it and accept appropriate help." Regardless of the point at which the learning disability or ADD (Attention Deficit Disorder) is identified, there are some common characteristics that can be noted.

Students with learning disabilities who were not formally identified during the undergraduate years are often diagnosed for the first time after they performed very poorly on one of the graduate entrance exams. It is not unusual for these students to have "failed" these exams several times before they search in desperation for an answer to the riddle: "How could I score so poorly given my solid undergraduate record, my preparation and intellectual abilities?" After a comprehensive diagnostic evaluation, these individuals are often relieved to find out that they have a legitimate disability that directly interferes with their performance on standardized examinations.

To the surprise of many graduate school faculty and administrators, a large proportion of LD and/or ADHD students in graduate and professional programs may not be identified until they experience the rigors of the graduate or professional school curriculum. Jordan (1995) recently commented at the twenty-fifth anniversary conference of the learning disabilities program at Curry College that "many believe that the term learning disabled graduate or professional student is an oxymoron which just cannot exist." Her point is well taken. Despite their high aptitudes, these students often have a history of performing relatively poorly on standardized tests and in-class exams. This history of uneven test performance is often discordant with written assignments that are completed outside of the classroom, such as term papers. Test performance often drops when they feel the pressures of the clock. This in turn results in heightened test anxiety which can magnify the effects of the learning disability. Additional time on exams provides students with learning disabilities the opportunity to selectively attend to information, to organize their thoughts, and to retrieve words from memory. A graduate student with a learning disability from Colgate University recently reflected upon his first year at law school by stating, "I benefited by learning an unsurpassable work ethic because to become successful in law I would have to work much harder and longer than other students. It was seriously disconcerting my first semester when I scored only a 2.24 GPA. I did not finish any of my first semester exams. I was told this was normal."

As previously mentioned, IQ scores are often in the average to gifted range, with the greatest difficulties noted on tests that tap into language processing abilities. Large discrepancies are often noted between reading and listening comprehension. Students frequently find that they can read technical material, but they don't remember what they have read. In some cases, problems with reading comprehension can be attributed to slow visual processing speed or decoding deficits. In other cases reading comprehension is directly affected by short-term memory problems. Some students with learning disabilities find their biggest problem with reading comprehension at the graduate level is that they interpret the information too literally. These students are often overwhelmed by the rapid pace of the program, the amount of assigned reading in graduate school and the amount of lecture material that must be quickly learned and integrated into practice. Written work is often characterized by significant problems with spelling, poor handwriting, and weak grammar skills. Writing a master's thesis or a doctoral dissertation is particularly challenging because many of these graduate students lack the day-to-day organizational and time management skills needed to budget their time effectively to meet long-standing deadlines. Retrieving and organizing large quantities of technical information from a large university library can be overwhelming. On the positive side, verbal abilities are often a high point for these students. Law students with strong verbal skills often gravitate to the courtroom and medical students with strong verbal abilities are often praised for their bedside manner and clinical abilities.

Graduate Students with Attention Deficit Disorders

Graduate students with ADD often have to contend with problems such as impulsivity, restlessness and a short attention span. In adults, ADD is often a "hidden disorder," with its symptoms obscured by problems with relationships, staying organized and holding a steady job. Many adults who are diagnosed as having ADD are first recognized as having problems with substance abuse or impulse control (Lerner, Lowenthal, & Lerner, 1995). Focusing attention in a classroom or in a science laboratory may be hampered by difficulties with selective attention, impulsivity, and a tendency to perseverate on a given task for too long. For students who do not exhibit excessive motor activity, and who appear inattentive, the ADD may be limited to problems with controlling the internal distractions of being bombarded with a wellspring of thoughts, facts and ideas.

Some graduate students with ADD seems to thrive on the stimulation found in fast-paced graduate programs where juggling multiple tasks are the norm. For others, the biggest challenge is not whether they can pay attention, but rather how they can effectively sustain their attention over time. As a result, more and more students are looking for effective treatments that may include therapy, medication, and counseling. Graduate school may prove to be a better place to find out one's best dosage for a given medication and patterns for use than in the working world where symptoms of dosage irregularities may result in being fired. Taking a stimulant medication, such as Ritalin or Dexedrine, it is often an option for these students as they search for a therapeutic method of treatment that will allow them to maximize their talents and abilities without disabling side effects. Barkley (1990) noted that the success rate for medical treatment is lower for adults than for children—about 50 percent for adults compared to about 70 percent for children. In addition, adults have to contend with the fact that the use of stimulant medications may be viewed by graduate school faculty and peers as a "crutch." As a society we are often reluctant to accept the fact that people in respected professional fields may need to rely on medication to assist them in traversing the course of their daily lives.

Perhaps the most notable factor that sets graduate students with learning disabilities or those with ADD apart from their undergraduate counterparts is that they are highly motivated to succeed and often hypersensitive about being "discovered" as having a disability. They don't want to appear "stupid" by asking too many questions in lectures, by depending on peers for assistance or appearing overly dependent on advisors or clinical instructors for guidance. As a result, they may feel isolated from their classmates. These feelings of isolation and inadequacy can undermine self-confidence and perpetuate feelings of shame and humiliation. They are often fearful that if they disclose their disability to an academic advisor or dean, that information may be used against them, discounted as not being real or, worst of all, shared openly in a departmental faculty meeting. One second year dental student recently commented that a faculty member told him that it would be better if he dropped out of the program "so at least we can get someone with better qualifications." Statements such as these can have a long lasting and demoralizing impact on students with learning disabilities enrolled in highly competitive professional programs.

Graduate Admissions Requirements

Given the steep competition in most graduate programs (e.g., law school, medical school, allied health professions) students with learning disabilities are often confronted with the dilemma of deciding whether or not to self-identify in the application process. Even though they may have graduated from a respectable undergraduate program and earned solid grades, they still have to demonstrate that they are otherwise qualified to meet the requisite standards for graduate school admission. Many students fear that graduate school admissions officers will look less favorably on applicants who elect to take their entrance examinations "under non-standardized conditions" versus applicants with a similar profile who do not disclose a disability and who take the exam in the conventional manner. Unlike procedures for admission at the undergraduate level, the admission process for graduate programs often varies widely within a given institution. It is often up to the individual department to determine its own standards and admissions criteria. This decentralized approach makes it difficult for prospective applicants with disabilities to determine the level of understanding and commitment that graduate admissions officers possess about disabilities and whether or not it is advisable to self-identify.

Graduate school admissions officers may find it especially difficult to assess on paper which applicants with LD are qualified for the rigors of medical or law school. They may realize that "standardized test measures don't tell it all," but they are often unclear as to how a learning disability or attention deficit disorder would affect future student performance in the graduate school curriculum. In such instances, it may be useful for graduate school admissions staff to confer with a learning disability specialist or psychologist who is knowledgeable and versed in working with these adults in order to gain further insight about a given applicant's prospects for success. Although admissions officers may not directly ask applicants if they have a disability in the initial stages of the admission process, they may ask an applicant to provide additional documentation of the disability and/or demonstrate how he/she will be able to fulfill essential course requirements with or without reasonable accommodations if the applicant asks for an accommodation (Essex-Sorlie, 1994; Helms & Helms, 1994). In 1982, the Council for Medical Education recommended that admissions committees place more emphasis on "personal qualities essential to the best practice of medicine, including warmth, a personal concern and even more importantly, integrity in both academic and interpersonal relationships." For applicants with learning disabilities who may not quite have the requisite Medical College Admission Test scores, but who possess personal qualities that make them good applicants, this perception by the Council on Medical Education is reassuring.

Frances Hall, (1995) the director of student programs for the Association of American Medical Colleges, points out that we need to "evaluate *ability* not their status as being disabled, while keeping in mind that we must not fundamentally alter the program or pose a threat to public safety." Ultimately, this means that admissions staff in conjunction with graduate school administrators have to define their "essential standards" and determine what limits need to be set as they seek to apply standards uniformly to all students. They need to ask, "What can be done to insure that we evaluate a student's true ability without the confines of disability-related factors?" and "What elements of the graduate school curriculum are non-negotiable or viewed as integral to the program of study?"

Once admitted, students with learning disabilities may feel compelled to demonstrate for themselves and to others that, with or without accommodations, they can meet legitimate program requirements and professional, licensing standards (Kincaid, 1992). Many first year graduate students believe that now that they are in their area of specialty (i.e., international banking, special education, or pediatrics), their learning disability won't affect them. Others believe that all they need to do is "buckle down" and study harder to get the results they desire. Students with ADHD may think that once their prescription medication takes effect they will be able to handle anything in graduate school. These misguided thoughts often result in students failing to meet performance standards by mid-semester and being referred to the academic support services offices.

Providing Academic Supports in Graduate School

Few graduate and professional school programs have direct access to a learning disability specialist on campus. Similarly, in the work world, few employees with learning disabilities have the opportunity to work closely with a specialist on the job. Although every company must have a human resource manager on site, these individuals are often more concerned about following union rules and company regulations than working with individuals with disabilities. Few employees with learning disabilities are aware of Employee Assistance Programs that can assist them in determining work adjustments that will enable them to perform the essential functions of a given job.

Typically, students who are experiencing academic problems are referred to the dean of student affairs who can determine whether the problems the student is having are minor or perhaps, more indicative of a pervasive learning disability. If an academic advisor or counselor believes that the presenting problem may be a learning disability or an attention deficit disorder, it may be appropriate to refer the student to a qualified professional for a comprehensive psycho-educational or neuropsychological evaluation. Adelman and Vogel (1991) emphasized that we are now in an "age of accountability"; therefore, evaluation will be increasingly mandated by legislation and government regulations. This need for accountability may encourage institutions to develop on-site diagnostic services. Although the cost of these services is substantial, the resulting consistency in the quality of diagnostic information assures the institution that students receiving specialized support have met clear eligibility criteria. An evaluation conducted by a licensed school psychologist or educational diagnostician will assume that the student receives consistent diagnostic services while also creating a standard that protects the institution (Behrens-Blake & Bryant, 1996).

It may be useful for service providers to establish some guidelines regarding what constitutes acceptable learning disability documentation and to determine what standards need to be met before an accommodation can be granted. Because of the variation in diagnostic procedures, differences in eligibility criteria, and disagreement in the interpretation of test results, there are valid concerns regarding the acceptance of some eligibility statements (Behrens-Blake & Bryant, 1996). It may be advisable to establish a timetable for the recency of the LD documentation. Many institutions follow a 3-5 year limit, given that the unique needs of students can change over time. Most graduate testing services adhere to the more conservative three-year limit and some are now requesting information on the credentials of the qualifying professional who conducted the evaluation. The prevailing practice is to accept documentation from medical doctors, licensed psychologists, neuropsychologists or learning disability specialists who have a history of reputable practice. The documentation should detail the exact nature of the student's disability, its severity, as well as specify the classroom accommodations or auxiliary aids that may be appropriate. A complete diagnostic report should include measures of cognitive ability, information processing, and academic achievement. All subtest scores should accompany the report. A specific diagnosis of a disability should be included; terms such as, "learning differences, " "slow reader" or "attention problems" do not constitute a documentable disability. If accommodations were not provided in the past, then the diagnostic report should state why accommodations were not necessary and why they are presently warranted.

Documentation of an attention deficit disorder, with or without hyperactivity, should be assessed in a comprehensive diagnostic interview by a qualified clinician. DSM-IV criteria for the three subtypes of ADD should be addressed as well as addressing any co-existing mood, behavioral, neurological, and/or personality disorders. A written report should describe and interpret the results of measures of attention, overall intelligence, spatial ability, language, memory, executive functioning, motor ability, and academic skills. The clinician should also make specific recommendations for further treatment, remediation, accommodations, and/or academic counseling, based upon the student's profile of strengths and weaknesses.

Academic support staff in graduate schools are often caught in the position of trying to advocate for students with disabilities while simultaneously being expected to respect a student's right to confidentiality, uphold and maintain rigorous technical standards, preserve core curriculum requirements, and safeguard the public trust. If students with learning disabilities are going to compete equitably in graduate or professional programs, it is essential that academic support staff understand learning disabilities as well as their responsibilities under the ADA for providing students with reasonable academic adjustments. Academic support staff may also need to further educate faculty members about these students, how they learn and their unique needs both in and out of the classroom. Academic support staff may request that they be invited to one of the regularly scheduled departmental meetings to discuss learning disabilities. An advantage of this approach is that accommodations and modifications particular to the specific disciplines can be discussed. Tomlan, Farrell and Geis (1990) have developed a sequenced model for the delivery of faculty in-service training beginning with large-group training, followed by staff development for individual departments, divisions or committees and ending with individual meetings with faculty who have students with disabilities in class. Academic support staff can tactfully encourage faculty members to create classroom settings that are more hospitable to the learning of all students by sharing a variety of different instructional methodologies and teaching approaches.

Faculty members may need to be reminded to keep regular office hours so they can meet with students to answer questions, clarify material or give feedback on class progress. It is particularly important that students with learning disabilities receive consistent, regular feedback throughout the semester so that they can utilize available campus resources to their advantage. Access to faculty can be improved if faculty have phone machines and e-mail so students can keep in close contact with their professors. Faculty should also make an effort to prepare their course syllabus in advance so that students who need taped materials can secure them in a timely fashion. The syllabus is an essential organizational tool for students with learning disabilities. Consequently, it should clearly state the expectations for the course, as well as guidelines with dates for papers, tests, and reading assignments. Faculty members should be encouraged to make a brief statement at the first class that they are happy to meet with students during office hours to discuss any special needs (Brinckerhoff, Shaw, & McGuire, 1993). At several institutions, including Barnard College and Ball State University, faculty invite students to share disability-related information by including a brief statement on all course syllabi. A typical statement may read, "If you need course adaptations or accommodations because of a documented disability, or if you have emergency medical information to share, please make an appointment during my office hours."

Brinckerhoff, Shaw and McGuire (1993) pointed out that faculty or teaching assistants who are on the front lines should be prepared to broach the subject of a suspected disability with students and to help by referring them to the academic dean or an academic counselor. They may be the first to address the issue by noting that a student appears to be highly motivated and yet, despite diligent effort, he/she is still performing below expectations. Faculty can assist in this process by describing their experiences with other bright students with learning disabilities with whom they have worked in the past or by offering to connect a newly identified student with a peer who has managed to successfully navigate the graduate curriculum despite his/her learning disability. Faculty should not trivialize a learning disability to be merely a "learning difference" or a "learning preference." They should emphasize that a learning disability is a disability that can be documented and is primarily concerned with how an individual takes in, sorts, retrieves, and expresses information and is no reflection of a lack of intelligence.

Determining Accommodations in Graduate Schools

Many graduate school administrators and faculty are becoming increasingly concerned about how to determine "reasonableness" in accommodating graduate students with disabilities. Some faculty members in graduate programs who are not aware of the ADA are reluctant to grant a student with a visual processing disorder additional time on an exam because "all students do better with additional time." Some law school faculty have expressed concerns about whether or not a practicing lawyer needs "split second decision making" in the courtroom or whether it is ethical for an attorney with dyslexia to "double bill" a client because it takes him twice as long to prepare a legal brief. Professor Laura Rothstein (1990) at the University of Houston School of Law challenges those faculty members who think that additional time gives students with learning disabilities an "unfair advantage. "She contends that there should be some limits to the amount of time granted and only students with the most severe disabilities should be permitted double time for exams and unlimited time is unlikely to be granted (Rothstein, 1990).

It is of utmost importance that faculty members maintain their academic standards but also remain open to listening to the needs of these students and seriously consider filling these requests. The students are often in the best position to articulate what types of accommodations they will need and what types of accommodations have been successful in the past. Accommodation amplifies the means for students with disabilities to achieve the desired end or standard required of all students (Jarrow, 1993). On occasion, the agreed-upon accommodations do not work out in the student's best interests. Under such circumstances, it is imperative that academic support staff assist the student in re-negotiating accommodations that will fill his or her needs effectively. This trial-and-error process can be unsettling to graduate school faculty, but if a collaborative team approach is used from the outset, the knowledge and attitudes of all constituencies can be enhanced. On the other side of the coin, students need to remember that faculty members are not bound to accept every accommodation requested and, in some instances, students are making a "leap to entitlement" by demanding a laundry list of accommodations that may not be appropriate. Brinckerhoff, Shaw and McGuire (1996) states that, given the heterogeneous nature of the college population with learning disabilities, requests for testing accommodations must be addressed on an individual basis. To provide blanket accommodations to all students is a disservice both to students whose strengths may mitigate against an accommodation in specific courses and to faculty who are pivotal in ensuring access while maintaining technical standards. There should always be a data-based connection between students' strengths and weaknesses and their eligibility for *specific* types of accommodations.

Recently several graduate and professional programs have developed standard accommodation policy statements regarding services for students with learning disabilities (University of California at Berkeley, 1995). Others have taken a broad sweeping approach and have developed technical standards which specifically state what skills a matriculated candidate must be able to demonstrate in order to complete a given curriculum (University of Tennessee-Memphis, 1995). Technical standards often focus on specific domains or skill areas that must be mastered in the practice of a given profession. In the field of medicine, for example, standards have been developed around the following areas: observation, communication, motor functioning, intellectual-conceptual, behavioral, and social attributes. For a more in-depth discussion of technical standards readers are advised to consult the AAMC publication, *The Americans with Disabilities Act and the Disabled Student in Medical School: Guidelines for Medical Schools* (1993).

Once admitted, it is the school's responsibility to provide "reasonable accommodations" and, in general, to pay the costs associated with the accommodation unless such expenses would be viewed as an unfair administrative or financial burden (Kincaid, 1995). When determining whether an accommodation is an undue financial hardship, the entire budget of the institution must be considered. Some accommodations that graduate schools might reasonably be expected to make for students with learning disabilities include course load modification and extended time for the completion of examinations, courses, thesis requirements and degree(s) (AAMC, 1993). Some graduate schools are more willing to experiment with meeting the accommodation needs of students. At Widener University, students have been permitted to use memory-free word processors to type exams, to sit in special chairs or at special tables to listen to tape recorded versions of exams and even to play a "white noise" tape to eliminate distractions during exams (Cleesattle & Seiberg, 1995). This individualized approach to accommodation was exemplified by a medical student with a learning disability from Dartmouth Medical School who stated, "I had also asked for a private place to take the exam, but because every course was different the second year, it was hard to ask for this special item with every course director (in fact, I never did the second year, but it would have been helpful if I did). What did help me instead was to put ear plugs in and have the space to spread out to take the exam..."

The following list of accommodations may be viewed as reasonable under the ADA, depending on the nature of the student's disability and the curriculum standards set by the graduate program:
• readers;
• additional time to complete tests, course work, and graduation requirements;
• rest breaks between test sessions;
• access to a dictionary or spell-checker;
• nonprogrammable calculator;
• word-processor for essays;

- individual testing rooms;
- permission to record answers in test booklets rather than on answer sheets;
- more than one test day;
- oral exams;
- proofreader;
- calculator with voice output;
- tape recorded version of exam;
- tape recorder for notetaking;
- notetaker in course lectures, assistive listening devices or tape recorder; and
- adaptations in instructional methods.

In addition to the above mentioned accommodations, Scott (1990, pp. 403-404) has generated a list of questions that may be useful for service providers to follow:

- Can the student with a learning disability meet all the essential program requirements when he or she is given reasonable accommodations?
- Will the accommodations provided pose any risk to personal or public safety?
- Are the proposed accommodations stipulated in writing in advance, and do they reflect the purpose of a program or course?
- What skills or competencies will be needed for graduation, licensing or certification?
- Which program elements are negotiable and which are not?

Success Takes Team Work

Providing academic adjustments to students with learning disabilities at the graduate and professional school level is a complex process that depends on the proactive efforts of administrators, support staff, faculty, and the students themselves. Policy makers need to establish procedures that legitimize the requests for accommodations on which students with disabilities depend (Brinckerhoff et al., 1993). Support staff need to learn more about the unique learning and psychosocial needs of this talented population of students who often have learning disabilities and are gifted. Faculty must acknowledge that students with learning disabilities can and do learn differently and must be willing to explore alternative ways of determining a student's proficiency with course materials without lowering standards. Ultimately, the key players in this process are the students with learning disabilities, who must be ready to demonstrate their willingness to take risks, to realistically assess their strengths and limitations and to select academic adjustments that will allow them to effectively compensate for their disability in graduate school and in the world of work.

Adapted from: Brinckerhoff, L.D., (1997). Students with Learning Disabilities in Graduate and Professional Programs: Emerging Issues on Campus and Challenges to Employment. In: *Learning Disabilities and Employment* by Paul J. Gerber and Dale S. Brown, Austin, TX: PRO-ED Publishers.

Chapter Eight

Communication Skills of Adults with Learning Disabilities

Noel Gregg, Ph.D.

Noel Gregg, Ph.D., is currently director of the University of Georgia Learning Disabilities Center, author of Written Expression Disorders, *co-author of* Assessment: The Special Educator's Role, *and co-editor of* Adults with Learning Disabilities: Theoretical and Practical Perspectives.

The term "learning disabilities" refers to a communication disorder impacting the acquisition of either verbal (e.g., words) or nonverbal (e.g., pictures, body language) symbols. Language (verbal and nonverbal) can be thought of as the rules governing semiotics, or the representation of ideas through symbols (Hoy & Gregg, 1994). These symbols can be words, pictures, or gestures. As Lyon (1975) noted, however, there is not always a clear dichotomy between verbal and nonverbal indices. To understand what someone says to us requires an interpretation of both the verbal and the nonverbal language he or she uses. The language or communication profiles of adults with learning disabilities are extremely heterogeneous and must always be evaluated in light of personal background, contexts, and demands (Wiig, 1996). Throughout the literature, a great deal of attention has been focused on the academic deficits of those with learning disabilities. While academics are certainly impacted by learning disabilities, the communication strengths and weaknesses of adults with learning disabilities need greater attention from professionals. The communication competencies of an individual will certainly affect his or her success across personal, academic, social, and vocational settings.

Adults with learning disabilities can learn to identify their communication strengths and weaknesses so that compensatory strategies, direct instruction, or accommodations can be provided to ensure success across different contexts. Without a better understanding of the communication disorders impacting their daily living, adults with learning disabilities often feel they have lost control (Wiig, 1996). The purpose of this chapter is to consider the profiles of two adults with learning disabilities (one with verbal and another with nonverbal learning disabilities) in order to illustrate some of the communication problems facing adults with learning disabilities.

A great deal of attention in the literature has recently been directed to adults with learning disabilities who demonstrate underlying phonological deficits that impact significantly on their ability to decode words for reading and spelling (Bruck, 1992; Podhajski, 1998). Phonological deficits are certainly present across a large percentage of adults with learning disabilities, but it is also important to recognize that these specific deficits are not indicative of the entire population. For some adults with learning disabilities, the cognitive and language deficits are not in the area of phonology. The purpose of this chapter is to focus on (verbal and nonverbal) language-based problems facing many adults with learning disabilities other than phonologically-based deficits.

Verbal Communication Disorders

The verbal communication strengths and weaknesses of the adult population with learning disabilities have not received sufficient attention from researchers and other professionals, despite evidence that language-based problems continue to interfere with the communicative success of the adult population (Blalock, 1987; Morris & Leuenberger, 1990; Wiig, 1996). Manifestations of verbal communication deficits, often subtle to begin with, become even subtler with increasing age (Wallach & Liebergott, 1984) and the patterns displayed are often different than those identified in children. In fact, the verbal language deficits of adults may be so subtle as to be interpreted by others as social eccentricities and/or the result of social skill deficits (Landa, Folstein & Isaacs, 1991). At times, traditional language assessment that focuses on isolated word and sentence levels fails to identify subtle, complex verbal language deficits demonstrated by adults. It becomes paramount for professionals who assess and provide support services to adults with learning disabilities to focus on the elusive interaction of cognitive, language, academic, and emotional issues while maintaining a viewpoint of multidimensional analysis.

Verbal communication consists of the ability to process language at the sub-word (phonological), sentence (syntax), word (semantics), and text (discourse) levels and to apply those skills in socially effective ways (pragmatics). As language users, we must be able to understand language (receptive skills) and produce it (expressive skills). Underlying our ability to understand and produce language are many cognitive abilities. Oral communication, in addition to pure language skills, requires the ability to plan and execute tasks directed toward goals (Hoy & Gregg, 1994). Some adults with learning disabilities demonstrate adequate expressive and receptive language skills when asked to use them in isolation, however, if they are required to use their skills in an integrated or organized manner, problems are identified. Behaviors noted when organization skills are impacted include difficulty monitoring one's own actions, focusing attention, planning ahead, and completing directions. Breakdowns can be noted across receptive, expressive, and organization abilities. Again, one must always keep in mind that past experiences with language and cultures significantly influence communication patterns and must at all times be considered when language competence is being evaluated.

A case study approach is going to be used throughout this chapter to illustrate the impact of communication disorders across different contexts (instructional, vocational, and social). For example, John is a 28-year-old male who works as a mechanic for Quick-Lube, an auto chain that specializes in oil changes and quick car maintenance. An evaluation of John's oral communication, identified his strengths and weaknesses, determined his functional limitations, and identified vocational, academic, and social training appropriate for someone like John whose profile represents a verbal communication disability.

• **John's Background Information** – John grew up in an intact middle class home in the southern part of the United States. He has two brothers who are college graduates and have no history of learning or emotional difficulties. John was identified in first grade as demonstrating a language/learning disability by the public school he attended. He subsequently was served by special education in both self-contained and resource programs. By the time John got to eighth grade, however, he felt school was too difficult and not helping him meet his vocational goals, therefore, when he reached the age of sixteen, he dropped out of school. After losing a series of jobs, John decided he would attend a local adult literacy center and obtain his GED. In addition, he reconnected with his local vocational rehabilitation counselor who worked very closely with him on both literacy and job placement. The vocational rehabilitation counselor insisted that John obtain an evaluation to assess the current impact of his language disabilities on his learning since this information could help in the development of job placement, accommodations, and modifications. The following information is obtained from what the literature tells us about verbal communication disorders across each of the areas assessed, as well as from an assessment of John's abilities.

• **The Literature and Cognitive Ability** –Adults with verbal communication disorders report specific linguistic and communicative difficulties across academic, social, and vocational settings, but they also report significant problem-solving difficulties (Klein, Moses & Altman, 1990). Investigating the abstract reasoning and problem-solving skills of adults with learning disabilities, Stone (1987) identified specific strategies used by these individuals that did not always support fluent communication. He found that adults with learning disabilities demonstrated difficulty organizing sequences of goals and sub-goals necessary for the outcome of solving problems. Such difficulties can be observed in the everyday functioning of adults with learning disabilities. For example, they often demonstrate significant difficulty troubleshooting problems, or meeting day-to-day challenges (e.g., organizing schedules for completing work assignments; identifying alternative solutions to finishing tasks on a job if interrupted by a co-worker; predicting solutions to daily problems prior to the development of a crisis). Therefore, it is likely that reasoning strategies (inductive and deductive reasoning) underlie some of the verbal communication deficits demonstrated by adults with learning disabilities. Researchers across disciplines continue to investigate the underlying information processing abilities required for understanding, remembering, and producing ideas (Ackerman, Kyllomen & Roberts, 1999). Future research will provide more information on the contribution those cognitive processes (such as working memory, executive functions, attention, and motor skills) make towards the ability to effectively communicate orally.

• **John's Cognitive Ability** – John found it hardest to solve problems using verbal language (e.g., similarities, analogies). He showed strengths in problem-solving when he could visually see a problem and utilize concrete aids to arrive at solutions. Weaknesses identified during his assessment across cognitive processing measures included difficulty remembering and attending to information when it was presented orally in the absence of a familiar context. During problem-solving, when he was provided with visual stimuli and a real-world context, John's success increased significantly.

• **The Literature on Oral Language** – The literature pertaining to the verbal communication strengths and weaknesses of adults with learning disabilities is extremely scarce and features very few empirically-based studies. Even researchers focusing on the phonological profiles of individuals with learning disabilities have produced only a small body of literature specific to the adult population. The areas of verbal communication that will be reviewed in this chapter relate to linguistic rule-learning, word-finding, semantics, discourse, and pragmatics.

Linguistic rule-learning is vital to our ability to comprehend and express language in sentences and discourse. There are rules that govern our ability to put words together in sentences and to relate words/ideas between sentences and across text. The linguistic rules that govern our ability to put words together in sentences are referred to as syntax. We must be able to effectively understand the relationships among the words we hear (receptive syntax) and order words in produced sentences (expressive syntax). Some adults with learning disabilities can understand sentence structure (receptive syntax), but have difficulty expressing words in sentences (expressive syntax). Other adults demonstrate the reverse problem with syntax and have more difficulty understanding sentence structure than producing it. Researchers have consistently found that many adolescents and adults with learning disabilities demonstrate difficulty in using syntactic rules to produce complex sentences (e.g., subordination of clauses and relative clauses) or maintaining the relationships between sentences (cohesion), such as problems with pronoun reference, demonstrative adjectives or transitions (Gregg, 1985; Semel, Wiig, & Secord, 1991; Wiig & Secord, 1992). Receptive and expressive oral syntax problems can affect an adult's listening comprehension, reading, written language, and social skill success. Common errors in the oral language of an adult with verbal syntax deficits would include omissions and substitutions of words as well as reversal of word order.

Closely connected to syntax and semantics is morphology. Words are constructed from basic units of meaning called morphemes, and the rules governing them are referred to as morphology. Common errors indicative of morphological disorders include omissions of plurals, possessives, tenses, word endings, and prefixes or suffixes. However, as with all areas of communication, an adult's word formation knowledge must always be evaluated against his or her dialectical background to determine if there is a language difference or disorder.

At the word level, adults with learning disabilities can have difficulty developing adequate vocabularies, using sarcasm, abstract words, indirect requests or multiple-meaning words. Litowitz (1987) found significant language and conceptualization issues facing adults with learning disabilities. She analyzed oral definitions given by adults with learning disabilities and observed the interface where conceptualization and language come together. The adults with learning disabilities in her study demonstrated linguistic strategies that are more common among young children in their attempts to define words, relying more on functional than Aristotelian definitions.

Verbal words are labels for thoughts, or as Vygotsky so eloquently stated, "thought may be compared to a cloud shedding a shower of words" (1962, p. 56). Concepts and linguistic rules underlie the labels we use for words. For instance, the word 'when' represents the concept of 'time' and is most often part of linguistic structures featuring adverbs, prepositional phrases, or tense markers. Another example might be the word 'where', which represents the concept of 'space' and is most often placed in adverbial prepositional phrases. An adult who demonstrates problems understanding the words 'when' or 'where' could have underlying conceptual difficulties with regard to space or time. Certainly, one can see how problems with words such as 'when' and 'where' might have an impact on social interactions or reading comprehension tasks. Also, it is not enough to know the denotative (and connotative) meanings of a word. Consider the verbs 'speak', 'say', 'talk', and 'tell'. All represent similar concepts, but their effective use requires a mastery of the grammatical constraints that apply to each."

A very common characteristic of adults with verbal communication disorders is their difficulty recalling words quickly (word-finding). Here the problem is expressive: the adult knows the word but cannot recall the label. Behaviors often noted when an individual demonstrates word-finding problems include overuse of nonspecific words, functional definitions, interjections, placeholders, as well as word and phrase repetitions to fill space resulting in disorganized text.

Discourse or narrative production is often difficult for adults with learning disabilities. Discourse requires using all the components of language (phonology, syntax, semantics, and pragmatics), as well as numerous extralinguistic and organizational skills, to communicate ideas. During the course of a day, we must engage many different discourse structures (e.g., conversations, stories, school discourse, work discourse), adjusting linguistic and extralinguistic aspects of our presentation depending on the needs and identity of the audience. With each discourse structure, an adult must engage in referencing, attending, and perspective-taking activities that will provide effective exchange of information (Hoy & Gregg, 1994).

Adults with learning disabilities often appear to understand and use basic story grammars, but they produce much shorter stories, less complete or abbreviated story episodes, and less sophisticated links between episodes than do their non-LD peers (Roth & Speckman, 1994). While the ability to tell stories orally may improve from adolescence to adulthood, many adults continue to experience difficulties. Because adeptness in oral language is vital to communication success, possible results of difficulties in oral communication include an inability to maintain employment, problems, difficulty building social associations or friendships, and failure in educational settings (Roth & Speckman, 1994).

Pragmatics refers to the rules governing the use of language in context. We use language across many different settings to negotiate many functions such as greeting others, regulating activities, exchanging information, expressing feelings, to imagining, and using metalinguistic strategies (Rees, 1988; Wiig, 1996).

• **John's Oral Language** – Oral language problems were apparent and associated with John's ability to understand vocabulary, to quickly name words (word-finding) and to produce conversation or narratives (discourse). His problems understanding the meaning of words were most pronounced when he was asked to use abstract or double-meaning words. In addition, he demonstrated great difficulty interpreting indirect requests. Significant problems were noted in John's ability to recall words, and his verbal communication was peppered with fillers and hesitations. At times, these problems appeared to impact his ability to keep his discourse organized for the listener. He also demonstrated problems with listening comprehension tasks and his ability to keep conversations and stories organized.

• **The Literature on Achievement** – Johnson (1987) suggests that cognitive and oral language processing deficits contribute to reading difficulties. A connection between reading comprehension and linguistic rule learning has been established by Cooper (1988) and others (Kintsch, 1977; Cox, Shanahan, & Sulzby, 1990). Better writers also tend to be better readers, which is consistent with the idea that knowledge of linguistic rules is part of general literacy acquisition, and that this knowledge is implicated in both reading comprehension and writing quality regardless of age or differences in genre.

  Verbal communication is a complex system that is intricately tied to literacy and schooling. While written language and oral language can be viewed as cultural and social processes (Englert, 1992; Englert & Mariage, 1991), they also are considered to be distinct forms of communication (Chafe & Danielewicz, 1987; Halliday, 1987; Horowitz & Samuels, 1987; Nystrand, 1987). Some researchers consider written speech more complex, more difficult, and more abstract than oral speech (Rieber & Carton, 1987-1997). In fact, it is a type of monologue during which the writer must fully explain the context of the situation and predict the needs of the audience in order for complete comprehension to occur. Writing also requires more volition and better organization of thoughts than speaking requires. Whereas a person may be internally motivated (based on the situation) to speak in order to communicate, motivation for writing often occurs externally in the form of an instructor's or employer's assignment (Rieber & Carton, 1987-1997). Therefore, the underlying verbal communication deficits are going to have a serious impact on the academic success of an individual.

• **John and Achievement** – Across achievement areas, specific problems were identified involving John's ability to understand what he reads (comprehension). He showed average performance when he was asked to read words in isolation (decoding). In the area of written expression, John's weaknesses were noted when he was required to write complex sentences or organize his sentences together into a text. On tasks measuring mathematics skills, John demonstrated average performance on calculation skills, but he showed below average performance when solving problems. The problem in mathematics appears to be related directly to language rather than mathematical reasoning.

The Literature on Social/Emotional Factors– The emotional adjustment of adults with learning disabilities has not received adequate attention from researchers. White (1992) reviewed the outcome studies of adults with learning disabilities and reported that of all the areas of adjustment investigated in those studies, social/emotional adjustment was given the least amount of attention. The concomitance of learning disabilities and emotional/behavioral disabilities is becoming more recognized by professionals (Rock, Fessler & Church, 1997). The comorbidity of learning disabilities and emotional/behavioral disabilities is startlingly high. For instance, Faigel, Doak, Howard, and Sigel (1992) reported that three-fourths of youth admitted to a psychiatric hospital inpatient unit for adolescents were learning disabled. A twenty-year longitudinal study (Raskind, Goldberg, Higgins & Herman, 1998) of adults diagnosed (as children) with learning disabilities found that 42 percent of the overall sample had experienced major psychological disturbances. An interesting aspect of the study was that the socio-economic status of the sample was largely upper-class and that 95 percent of the individuals had attempted college. What has not been empirically studied is the impact of specific communication disorders on the social and emotional development of individuals. At the present time, adults with learning disabilities and professionals working with them must rely solely on clinical observations to hypothesize about the connections between communication disorders and emotional well being.

• **John and Social/Emotional Factors** – John's difficulties using and understanding language have impacted his social skills. His concrete interpretation of language and difficulty processing language in a timely manner often cause him to miss social cues. He appears very literal and responds slowly to social situations. In addition, he may demonstrate problems understanding sarcasm, double-meaning words, jokes, and indirect requests. Ongoing word-finding problems interfere with the usual conversational give-and-take so common to social conversation, leading to feelings of social isolation. Due to his social isolation, John demonstrated a tendency toward depression. Social skill training will need to focus on developing strategies for interacting socially given his significant oral language problems.

Conclusion

John's verbal communication disability impacts and functionally limits him in the areas of abstract verbal reasoning, oral communication, academic achievement, and social skills. The types of work environments that John should avoid include highly verbal jobs (both for understanding and expressing language), academically demanding jobs requiring extensive reading or writing, and environments with high demands with regard to social interaction. Based on John's evaluation, we could predict that he would experience instructional and vocational problems in the following areas:

1. Remembering and understanding information that is presented only in an auditory manner.
2. Remembering information that is presented quickly and as new iso-

lated information presented without a context. For example, phone numbers, dates, or facts presented in class, directions, vocabulary words, or isolated concepts presented in training.
3. Learning the meaning of new words.
4. With memory or achievement strategies for instruction, social, or employment purposes based on a difficult vocabulary level and unfamiliar words.
5. Understanding conversations, stories, or lectures.
6. Timed projects, tasks, or tests, especially those requiring the use of verbal language.
7. Jobs or assignments that require extensive reading and writing.
8. Solving mathematical word problems.
9. Interacting with peers at school or work.
10. Making and keeping friends.

For a professional working with John or any adult with a verbal learning disability, there are several general strategies that will enhance learning and communication. Table 1 delineates these guidelines. It is imperative that John understand these strategies so that he can help others working with him to better facilitate communication. In addition, specific pragmatic instruction would be recommended to address some of the social skill difficulties John is experiencing. Again, John's oral language deficits (i.e., word finding, abstract language, speed of processing, and organization) must be recognized in the development of any social skill program. It would also be important that John seek counseling to address his depression. Table 2 contains some assistive technology and Table 3 offers some low technology that would provide helpful accommodations and instructional strategies for John.

Table 1
General Strategies for Adults with Verbal Communication Disorders

Strategies
- Keep oral language simple and to the point. Statements and directions "subject-verb-object" (e.g. "Park the car in the garage." "Bring the groceries into the kitchen and put them away." NOT "Before you bring the groceries in the kitchen to put away, I want you to park the car in the garage at the back of the building.")

- Keep printed material simple and to the point – instructions, pamphlets, books, manuals, letters, and memos.

- Use familiar language for instruction with concrete examples.

- Explain any new words with examples and definitions related to the topic (or context).

- Restrict written materials (memos, directions, letters, and lessons) to one or two ideas per page.

- Allow time for a person to "collect thoughts" before answering or presenting an idea. Some need to write everything out first.

- Set off important ideas using "bullets", numbers, underlining, or a different color. Highlight main ideas so they can be seen quickly.

- Avoid sarcasm or indirect requests.

- Avoid figurative language.

- Encourage a person to repeat or rephrase requests to ensure information was understood.

Table 2
Verbal Communication Disorders

Select Accommodations and Modifications
High Technology

ACCOMMODATIONS	I**	E**	S/E**
1. Voice activated programs	X	X	X
2. Word processing programs (color coding and voice)	X	X	X
3. Word prediction programs	X	X	X
4. CD-ROM Dictionary and Thesaurus	X	X	X
5. CD-ROM programs	X	X	X
6. Interactive-video if language problems are considered	X	X	X
7. Semantic organizers	X	X	

      **I   = Instructional Accommodations
      E   = Employment Accommodations
      S/E = Social/Emotional Accommodations

Table 3
Verbal Communication Disorders

Select Accommodations and Modifications
Low Technology

ACCOMMODATIONS	I**	E**	S/E**
1. Provide reader	X	X	
2. Provide modified books on tape	X	X	X
3. Provide notetaker	X	X	
4. Provide extension of time on oral response, reading and written expression tasks	X	X	
5. Provide hand held spellers	X	X	
6. Provide extension of time double time)	X	X	
7. Provide organization (sequence) for a task to be completed	X	X	
8. Provide information presented in context	X	X	X
9. Provide semantic mapping for reading and written expression	X		
10. Provide information presented in a visual format i.e., graphs, tables, pictures)	X	X	X
11. Provide oral or written directions that require modifications (for example, written with vocabulary and syntax at his level or using symbols). In addition, directions or lectures should avoid the use f sarcasm, indirect requests, and double-meaning words.	X	X	X
12. Provide activities that stress hands-on demonstrations of knowledge (for example, videos, films, or role-playing).	X	X	X
13. Provide information holistically in auditory or visual formats.	X	X	X
14. Provide frequent opportunities or the learner to paraphrase to ensure accuracy of information being processed.	X	X	X
15. Provide formats that avoid fill-in-the-blank or multiple choice formats.	X	X	

**I = Instructional Accommodations
E = Employment Accommodations
S/E = Social/Emotional Accommodations

Nonverbal Communication

Nonverbal communication refers to the attachment of meaning to symbols that are not verbal, such as the development of concepts related to space, time, touch, and nonverbal planning or organization. Nonverbal communication requires the ability to attend to, remember, analyze, organize, and synthesize nonverbal information in context. Competence with nonverbal abilities is crucial to obtaining success in everyday life. As an adult, even greater demands on nonverbal processing and reasoning are expected for even minimal success in the vocational and social worlds. Studies addressing adults with nonverbal disabilities describe individuals with severe adaptive and vocational limitations, emotional instabilities, social inadequacies, tendencies to panic in problem-solving situations, and heavy reliance on others for support (Jackson, 1988; Strang & Rourke, 1985; Rourke, Young, Strand & Russell, 1986). The subgroup of adults with nonverbal communication deficits has been of interest to researchers over the years, generating numerous diagnostic categories (e.g., nonverbal learning disabilities, Asperger's Syndrome, Pervasive Developmental Disorders, etc.).

Nonverbal communication, separate from the disability, has received extensive examination by researchers (Argyle, 1969; Argyle & Cook, 1976; Birdwhistle, 1952, 1970; Harper, Wren & Matarzzo, 1978). Such studies across many different disciplines reveal that language users access a sophisticated network of communication skills that includes kinetics (body language,), facial expression, paralanguage (tone of voice, sighs, cries), proxemics (use of space), and chronemics (use of time). As with verbal communication, each of these areas can operate in isolation and/or together.

The adult with nonverbal learning disabilities often demonstrates a discrepancy between certain verbal and nonverbal communication skills. Hoy and Gregg (1994) note the importance of observing whether the speaker's oral language matches his or her nonverbal language comprehension and expression. Adults with nonverbal learning disabilities often do not understand the meaning attached to disapproving looks or gestures (i.e., looking at one's watch to end a conversation) unless such nonverbal language is accompanied by verbal communication. When considering nonverbal communication abilities (just as with verbal skills), one must be sensitive to an adult's age, experiences, socioeconomic level, and cultural background.

Rita, a twenty-three year old female who is receiving services through vocational rehabilitation is an example of the impact of nonverbal communication disorders. An evaluation of Rita's abilities identified her strengths and weaknesses, determined her functional limitations, and identified the appropriate vocational, academic, and social training needed.

• **Rita's Background Information** – Rita is currently 23- years-old and receiving services through vocational rehabilitation. Her difficulties were first identified in third grade and she participated in special education under the categories of both learning disabilities and, later, behavior disorders. Despite attempts by the special education and rehabilitation professionals working with Rita during high school, she was unable to receive a regular graduation diploma. Since graduation, she has been unable to maintain any degree of employment.

The Literature and Cognitive Ability – The limited amount of empirical research investigating the abilities of adults with nonverbal learning disabilities has documented that these individuals often demonstrate cognitive problems in perception, analysis, organization, and synthesis of nonverbal information (Johnson, 1987; Myklebust, 1975; Rourke, 1995). Rourke (1995) identified other characteristics of this population, such as difficulty with complex psychomotor skills, difficulty with novel learning, problems attending to tactile and visual input, difficulty with physical exploratory behavior, memory of tactile, visual, or nonverbal information, and difficulty with hypothesis testing.

A frontal cortex system dysfunction has been proposed as an area of breakdown related to nonverbal disabilities. Stuss (as cited in Rourke, 1989) suggested that the frontal systems of the brain are of vital importance to executive control in novel situations. He went so far as to propose that the ability to self-reflect, analyze, and synthesize are core functions of the frontal cortex. These abilities are often inadequate among the population with nonverbal learning disabilities. Similarities between the executive functioning deficits demonstrated by individuals with ADHD and individuals with nonverbal learning disabilities are of recent interest to researchers. Fuster (as cited in Harnishfeger and Bjorklund, 1994) states that "the frontal lobes are involved in central executive functions, such as planning and monitoring performance, with a rich pattern of connections between the sensory and motor areas meeting the front lobes" (p, 17). Executive functioning deficits such as planning and monitoring performance have been identified as common among adults with learning disabilities.

• **Rita and Cognitive Ability** – Rita demonstrated difficulty with nonverbal reasoning that over the years has also impacted abilities needed to perform verbal reasoning tasks. She had particular problems with cognitive flexibility, making inferences (inferential reasoning), generalizing from task to task and setting to setting, and responding to new or unfamiliar situations (novelty). However, on rote, repetitive tasks (which Rita has experience performing), she was comfortable and did quite well. Rita was better able to solve problems that followed a rote, sequential order. Unordered or holistic problem-solving was very difficult for Rita.

Weaknesses in cognitive processing were apparent when Rita had to process information that was presented visually. Significant deficits were noted in her ability to discriminate differences between and among items that were visually similar. She found it extremely difficult to process and quickly scan symbols that were nonverbal in nature (i.e., pictures, charts, and diagrams). Significant problems were also noted in her ability to mentally manipulate information (for example, repeating information in an opposite order or solving a task requiring one to reverse steps in a process).

Rita also had problems recognizing the differences among environmental sounds and signals (for example, a ringing phone or a car horn) and various levels of intonation and pitch (in English, variation in pitch and intensity of the voice gives the emotional meaning of the message being communicated). In addition, significant deficits were noted on tasks requiring visual-spatial ability and fine motor skills. Cognitive strengths were noted with short-term memory requiring the recall of rote, verbal information presented orally (for example, remembering lists of words or increasingly longer sentences).

• **The Literature and Oral Language** – The oral language abilities of adults with learning disabilities has certainly been ignored. The focus of researchers has centered on understanding the cognitive strengths and weaknesses of this population. Yet, the intricate connection between verbal and nonverbal processing must again be emphasized. Deficits in either domain can impact the effectiveness of the other. For years, clinicians have reported that individuals with nonverbal learning disabilities appear to have an uncommon reliance on language as a primary tool of adaptation, despite the fact they often are inefficient language users (Jackson, 1988; Johnson & Myklebust, 1967). One of the best ways to examine the oral communication abilities of individuals with nonverbal learning disabilities is through their use of language in dialogue (Gregg & Jackson, 1989). Vygotsky (1962) felt that all forms of higher mental functions are the result of internalized social relationships. He proposed that all interpsychological processes are internalized to intrapsychological processes by egocentric speech, leading to inner language. One of the functions of inner language, then, is to help plan and regulate human action. Some of the difficulties adults with nonverbal language disabilities have maintaining meaningful dialogue clearly illustrate problems with the use of regulatory strategies.

Gregg and Jackson (1989) conducted an in-depth, qualitative study to explore the dialogue patterns of adults with learning disabilities. They identified four language patterns typical of the adults they studied. These patterns include monologic rather than dialogic speech acts, disorganized text, dependence on rehearsed stories, and difficulties using inner language as a self-regulatory tool. This study clearly illustrated the interaction of cognitive and language abilities with regard to communication. Dialogic speech requires the use of kinetic cues, abbreviated linguistic codes, and sensitivity to one's audience. In addition, language requires self-regulating, planning and organizational skills controlled by the executive functioning areas of the brain. Clearly, one can summarize the literature by stating that adults with nonverbal learning disabilities often demonstrate problem-solving, self-regulatory, and metapragmatic language deficits that have significant impacts on their vocational and personal lives.

• **Rita and Language** – In the area of oral communication, Rita demonstrated a relative strength in vocabulary. However, oral communication problems were noted which interfered with conversation (discourse) and pragmatic abilities. Rita found it difficult to organize what she wanted to say in a way that took into account the listener's requirements for understanding her message. Closely aligned to these problems was her difficulty using language appropriately in social situations (pragmatics). Rita often interrupted people, provided vague references in conversation, and failed to notice inadequate cohesion between ideas in conversations. In addition, her spatial orientation problems limited her ability to judge appropriate distances during conversation. She often stood too close to or too far away from people, making conversation difficult and uncomfortable for the conversation partner.

The Literature on Achievement – The academic deficits, more typical of individuals with nonverbal learning disabilities, appear to be in the areas of motor skills (gross and fine), written language (spelling, organization, and sense of audience), mathematics (calculation and applied problem-solving), and reading comprehension (Johnson & Mykelbust, 1967; Rourke, 1995). However, these individuals often do not demonstrate difficulties with the phonological processes involved in learning to read single words. Often, such individuals can appear to be able to read (orally) text beyond their comprehension level (hyperlexia). The majority of research on the achievement abilities of adults with learning disabilities comes from clinical descriptions or the child literature.

• **Rita and Achievement** – Across achievement areas, specific cognitive reasoning problems interfered with Rita's ability to gain information from reading if understanding required any degree of inferential reasoning or problem-solving. While her decoding (single-word reading) skills were appropriate for her ability level, her reading comprehension and written text were significantly impacted. On writing tasks, Rita not only had difficulty organizing her ideas but also exhibited problem remaining sensitive to the needs of the reader. The same problem she demonstrated with oral language (adjusting her language patterns to the audience–pragmatics) showed up in written language as a poor sense of audience. However, her lowest area of achievement was in mathematics both with calculation and applied problem-solving.

• **The Literature and Social/Emotional Factors** – Studies on adults with nonverbal learning disabilities describe individuals with severe, social adaptive limitations, emotional instabilities, social inadequacies, tendencies to panic in novel problem-solving situations, and heavy reliance on others for support (Jackson, 1988; Strang & Rourke, 1985; Rourke, 1995; Rourke, Young, Strang & Russell, 1986). Certainly, it is easy to recognize how a breakdown in processing nonverbal symbols (pictures, body language, intonation) would significantly impact social skills. In addition, problems with executive functions that control self-regulatory behavior, planning, and organizing would similarly make social interaction very difficult. As adults, these individuals are at risk for internalized psychological disorders such as depression, anxiety, and dissociative disorders.

• **Rita and Social/Emotional Factors** – Rita's difficulties extended to interpersonal (social) signals as well. She demonstrated significant problems interpreting the meaning of facial and hand gestures, interpersonal distance, and other elements of body language. Rita's processing difficulties with nonverbal language (for example, body language, facial cues) have impacted her social skills. In addition, due to her slow speed of processing and difficulty with motor tasks, social interaction often produces negative consequences (criticism, ridicule). Ongoing difficulties organizing information, orienting herself in space, and managing time have led to problems across instruction, employment, and social settings. Living with these significant deficits her entire lifetime have contributed to manifestations of depression and anxiety.

Conclusion

Rita's nonverbal communication disabilities impact and functionally limit her in the areas of reasoning, cognitive flexibility, speed of processing, oral communication (dialogue and pragmatics), academic achievement, and social skills. The types of work environments that Rita should avoid include highly busy and interactive settings requiring quick decision-making or flexibility. Based on Rita's evaluation, we identified that she would experience instructional and vocational problems in the following areas:

1. Problem solving using nonverbal reasoning (interpreting meaning from pictures, graphs, symbols presented with icons, and determining differences in environmental sounds).
2. Problem solving using verbal reasoning (inferential reasoning, generalization, learning new tasks, and cognitive flexibility).
3. Understanding and using appropriate social skills (tonal intonation, body language, facial gestures, understanding appropriate personal space and spatial relations).
4. Social interactions such as making and keeping friends.
5. Visual discrimination and quickly scanning materials.

6. Performing tasks that require fine motor skills.
7. Performing tasks quickly.
8. Organizing conversational speech and understanding appropriate speech to use with various listeners.
9. Tasks that require reading and writing.
10. Mathematical problem solving.
11. Organization of school, work, and personal activities.
12. Keeping track of time, meeting due dates for projects, keeping appointments, and getting lost or not being able to follow directions.
13. Depression.
14. Anxiety.

For a professional working with Rita or any adult with nonverbal learning disabilities, there are several general strategies that will enhance learning and communication. Table 4 lists these strategies. It is imperative that Rita begin to understand these strategies so that she can relate them to those working with her and better facilitate communication. Table 5 contains some suggested assistive technology appropriate for Rita and Table 6 provides a list of low technology suggestions for working with an individual demonstrating nonverbal learning disabilities.

Table 4
General Strategies for Adults with Nonverbal
Communication Disorders

Strategies
- Observe the individual's behavior closely, especially in novel or otherwise complex situations. Focus on what the adult does rather than what he/she says.

- Assess cognitive strengths and weaknesses. Carefully analyze "verbal" abilities.

- Develop a systematic "step-by-step" instructional system. Parts-to-whole verbal teaching approach.

- Require verbal feedback from the adult. Discuss why the adult perceives he/she is "victimized". Discuss discrepancies between perceptions. Allow the adult to teach the instructor.

- Teach strategies for troublesome problem situations.

- Analyze very carefully the task/job competencies.

- Teach the generalization of learned strategies.

- Teach nonverbal behaviors (visual and auditory).

- Facilitate structured "group" interactions.

- Work with adult's significant others to help him/her gain insight and direction (parent groups, employer, friends).

- Carefully explore the issues of: egocentricity, consequences of rejection, manipulation.

Table 5
Nonverbal Communication Disorders

Select Accommodations and Modifications
High Technology

ACCOMMODATIONS	I**	E**	S/E**
1. Modified keyboards	X	X	
2. Modified mouse pads	X	X	
3. Voice activated programs	X	X	
4. Computerized calendar	X	X	X
5. Word prediction programs	X	X	
6. Interactive video for math, social skill, and employment program	X	X	X
7. Talking calendar	X	X	X
8. Organizers	X	X	X
9. Word processing programs	X	X	X
10. Switches	X	X	
-String Switches - Push Switches			
- Flex Switches - Grasp Switches			

**I = Instructional Accommodations
E = Employment Accommodations
S/E = Social/Emotional Accommodations

Table 6
Nonverbal Communication Disorders

Select Accommodations and Modifications
Low Technology

ACCOMMODATIONS	I**	E**	S/E**
1. Provide extension of time on tasks	X	X	X
2. Provide utilization of verbal directions (oral or written)	X	X	
3. Provide frequent opportunities for the learner to paraphrase to ensure accuracy of information being processed	X	X	X
4. Provide tasks broken into small, sequential steps	X	X	X
5. Provided directions or lectures should avoid the use of sarcasm, indirect request, and double meaning words	X	X	
6. Encourage the learner to utilize self-vocalization during problem solving tasks	X	X	X
7. Provide notetakers	X	X	
8. Provide a job coach		X	
9. Verbal labels should be identified to help with directionality	X	X	X
10. Provide daily management plans	X	X	X
11. Provide a set schedule for work schedules and school assignments	X	X	X
12. Provide social cues delivered verbally and not depend solely on nonverbal cues (for example, facial gestures)	X	X	X

**I = Instructional Accommodations
  E = Employment Accommodations
S/E = Social/Emotional Accommodations

Summary

Verbal and nonverbal communication has clearly not received enough attention from researchers in the field of learning disabilities, despite the recognized impact disabilities in these areas can have on the personal, instructional, and vocational success of adults. John and Rita have provided us with clear examples of the ways cognitive, linguistic, academic, and social/emotional behaviors are intertwined in learning, as well as how a breakdown across any of these areas impacts the other processes. Professionals need significantly more training in better understanding the communication (verbal and nonverbal) abilities and disabilities of the adult population with learning disabilities if they are to adequately provide services. The time has come to stop focusing only on behaviors and to better understand the underlying communication disorders complicating day-to-day activities for many adults with learning disabilities. The risk of continuing to ignore the communication disorders of the adult population with learning disabilities is reflected in the figures related to the social/emotional comorbidity of many of these individuals. Adults with communication disorders are our best guides in trying to better understand learning disabilities. Professionals must begin to listen more carefully and then act by producing more qualitative and empirically-based research with the outcome leading to more effective assessment and instruction for these individuals.

REFERENCES

Zimmerman

Fennell, E. B. (1995). The role of neuropsychological assessment in Learning Disabilities. *Journal of Child Neurology*, 10 (Supplement), S36-S41.

Gaddes, W. H. and Edgell, D. (1994) *Learning disabilities and brain function: A neuropsychological approach.* New York: Springer Verlag.

Gardener, H. (1983) *Frames of mind: The theory of multiple intelligences.* New York: Basic Books.

Gerber, P. J., Schneiders, C. A., Paradise, L. V., Reiff, H. B., Ginsberg, R. and Popp, P. A. (1990). Persisting problems of adults with learning disabilities: Self-reported comparisons from their school-age and adult years. *Journal of Learning Disabilities*, 23, 570-573.

Kaplan, Carol, Schacter, Emily (1991). Adults with undiagnosed learning disabilities: Practice Considerations. *Families in Society,* 72 (4), 195- 201.

Pennington, Bruce F. (1991). *Diagnosing learning disorders.* New York: Guilford Press.

Rourke, B. P. (1985). *Neuropsychology of learning disabilities: Essentials of subtype analysis.* New York: Guilford Press.

Silver, Larry (1990). Attention deficit-hyperactivity disorder: Is it a learning disability or a Related Disorder? *Journal of Learning Disabilities,* 23 (7), 394-397.

Spreen, O. (1989). Long term sequelae of learning disability: A review of outcome studies. In D. J. Bakker and H. van der Vlugt (eds.) *Learning disabilities: Vol. I. neurological correlates and treatment.* Amsterdam, Swets and Zeitlinger.

Vogel, S. A. (1989). Special Considerations in the Development of Models for Diagnosis of Adults with Learning Disabilities. In L Silver (Ed.), *The Assessment of Learning Disabilities.* Boston: Little Brown.

Riley

Adelman, P. B., & Wren, C. T. *Learning disabilities, graduate school, and careers: The student's perspective.* Lake Forest, IL: Barat College.

Aksamit, D., Morris, M., & Leuenberger, J. (1987). Preparation of student services professionals and faculty for serving learning-disabled college students. *Journal of College Student Personnel*, 28(1), 53-59.

Americans with Disabilities Act of 1990, 42 U.S.C.A., 12101 et seq. (West 1990).

Alster, E. H. (1997). The effects of extended time on algebra test scores for college students with and without learning disabilities. *Journal of Learning Disabilities, 30*(2), 222-227.

Baker, J. & Zigmond, N. (1990). Are regular education classes equipped to accommodate students with learning disabilities? *Exceptional-Children, 56*(6), 515-526.

Barkley, R. A. (1997). Behavioral inhibition, sustained attention, and executive functions: Constructing a unifying theory of ADHD. *Psychological-Bulletin, 121*(1), 65-94.

Dalton, B., Tivnan, T., Riley, M., Rawson, P., & Dias, D. (1995). Revealing competence: Fourth-grade students with diverse learning needs show what they know through paper-and-pencil and hands-on science performance assessments. *Learning Disabilities: Research and Practice, 10*(4), 198-214.

Fuchs, D., Roberts, P., Fuchs, L., Bowers, J. (1996). Reintegrating students with learning disabilities into the mainstream: A two-year study. *Learning-Disabilities-Research-and-Practice. 11*(4), 214-229.

Gordon, S. M., Riley, M. K., & Swanson, H. L. (1996, February). *Assessing and synthesizing research interventions for students with mild to moderate disabilities in regular and special education classrooms.* Paper presented at the meeting of the Pacific Coast Research Conference, San Francisco, CA.

Guckenberger v. Boston University, 974 F. Supp. 106 (D. Massachusetts 1997).

Hughes, C. A. & Smith, J. O. (1990). Cognitive and academic performance of college students with learning disabilities. *Learning-Disability-Quarterly, 13*(1), 66-79.

Individuals with Disabilities Education Act of 1990, 20 U.S.C. * 1400 et seq. (National Association of State Directors of Special Education 1997).

Lenz, K., Schumaker, J., Deshler, D., Fuchs, D., Fuchs, L., Gordon, S., Morocco, C., Riley, M., Schumm J. & Vaughn, S. (1995). *Planning for Academic Diversity in America's Classrooms: Windows on Reality, Research, Change, and Practice.* Lawrence, Kansas: Center for Research on Learning.

Leyser, Y. (1989). A survey of faculty attitudes and accommodations for students with disabilities. *Journal of Postsecondary Education and Disability, 7*, 97-108.

Mangrum, C. T., & Strichart, S. S. (Eds.). (1988). *College and the learning disabled student: Program development implementation and selection* (2nd ed.). Orlando, FL: Grune & Stratton.

Martin, R. (1992). *Continuing challenges in special education law.* Urbana, IL: Research Press.

Minner, S., & Prater, G. (1984). College teachers' expectations of LD students. *Academic Therapy, 20*(2), 225-229.

Morocco, C., Riley, M., Gordon, S., & Howard, C. (1995). *The Elusive Individual in Teachers' Planning.* In Ed. G. Brannigan, Chapter 8, *The Enlightened Educator*, New York: McGraw-Hill, 154-176.

Nealon, P. (1997, August 16). BU loses suit brought by students. *The Boston Globe*, pp. B1, B8.

Patton, J. R., & Polloway, E. A. (Ed.). (1996). *Learning disabilities: The challenges of adulthood.* Austin, TX: Pro-Ed.

Riley, M. K. (1991, October). *Valuing Cognitive Diversity in Teaching and Learning: Identifying Cognitive Strengths of the Diverse Learner.* Paper presented at the Harvard Graduate School of Education, Cambridge, MA.

Riley, M. K., Morocco, C. C., Gordon, S. M, and Howard, C. (1993). "Walking the Talk: Putting Constructivist Thinking into Practice in Classrooms." *Educational Horizons* , 71(4), 187-196.

Riley, M. K. (1996, April). *Looking at the ways varied assessment formats facilitate and obstruct the information processing of students with learning disabilities.* Paper presented at the annual meeting of the American Educational Research Association, New York, NY.

Riley, M. K. (1998). Leveling the playing field: Students with learning disabilities enjoying their competence, working hard and having fun in college. In Ed. T. Citro, Chapter 9, *The Experts Speak to Parents of Students with Learning Disabilities.* Boston: Learning Disabilities Association of Massachusetts.

Roberts, R. & Mather, N. (1995). Legal protections for individuals with learning disabilities: The IDEA, Section 504, and the ADA. *Learning-Disabilities-Research-and-Practice, 10*(3), 160-168.

Runyan, M. K. (1991). The effect of extra time on reading comprehension scores for university students with and without learning disabilities. *Journal of Learning Disabilities, 24*(2), 104-108.

Vogel, S. A., & Adelman, P. B. (1992). The success of college students with learning disabilities: Factors related to educational attainment. *Journal of Learning Disabilities, 25*(7), 430-441.

Wiig, E., & Semel, E. (1984). *Language Assessment and Intervention for Learning Disabled Children.* Columbus, Ohio: Charles E. Merrill.

Brinckerhoff

Adelman, P. B., & Vogel, S. A. (1991). The learning disabled adult. In B. Wong (Ed.), *Learning about learning disabilities*. (pp. 563-594). New York: Academic Press.

Association of American Medical Colleges (1993). *The Americans with Disabilities Act (ADA) and disabled students in medical school: Guidelines for medical schools*. Washington, D.C.: Author.

Barkley, R. A. (1990). *Attention deficit hyperactivity disorders: A handbook for diagnosis and treatment*. New York: Guilford Press.

Bateman, B. (1992). Learning disabilities: The changing land-scape. *Journal of Learning Disabilities, 25*, 29-36.

Behrens-Blake, & Bryant, B. (1996). Assessing student with learning disabilities in postsecondary settings. In J. Patton & E. Polloway (Eds.)., *Learning disabilities: The challenges of adulthood* (pp. 93-136). Austin, TX: PRO-ED.

Brinckerhoff, L. C., Shaw, S. F. & McGuire, J. M. (1993). *Promoting postsecondary education for students with learning disabilities: A handbook for practitioners*. Austin, TX: PRO-ED.

Brinckerhoff, L. C., Shaw, S F. & McGuire, J. M. (1996). Promoting access, accommodations, and independence for college students with learning disabilities. In J.R. Patton & E.A. Polloway (Eds.), *Learning disabilities: The challenges of adulthood* (pp. 71-92). Austin, TX: PRO-ED.

Brinckerhoff, L. (1991). Developing learning disability support services with minimal resources. *Journal of Postsecondary Education and Disability. 9* (1), 184-196.

Cleesattle, J., & Seiberg, J. (1995, Fall). Leveling the playing field? *Postsecondary Disability Network News, 25*, 1 ,2, 7.

Essex-Sorlie, D. (1994, July). The Americans with Disabilities Act: History, summary and key components. *Academic Medicine. 69* (7), 519-535.

Gerber, P. J. & Reiff, H. B. (1991). *Speaking for themselves: Ethnographic interviews with adults with learning disabilities*. Ann Arbor: University of Michigan Press.

Gerber, P. J. & Reiff, H. B. (1994). Perspective on adults with learning disabilities. In P. Gerber & H. Reiff (Eds.), *Learning disabilities in adulthood* (pp. 3-9) Austin, TX: PRO-ED.

Gerber, P. J., Ginsberg, R. J., & Reiff, H. B. (1992). Identifying alterable patterns in employment success for highly successful adults with learning disabilities. *Journal of Learning Disabilities, 25*, 475-487.

Hall, F. (1995, January). *Students with learning disabilities in medical school*. Presentation at Boston University School of Medicine conference, Boston, MA.

Hammill, D. D. (1990). On defining learning disabilities: An emerging consensus. *Journal of Learning Disabilities, 10*, 39-46.

Helms, L. B. & Helms, C. M. (1994, July). Medical education and disability discrimination: The law and future implications. *Academic Medicine. 69*, 535-543.

Information from HEATH. (1995, June/July). *Facts you can use: College freshmen with disabilities*. (p.6). Washington, D.C.: Author.

Jarrow, J. E. (1993, Winter). Beyond ramps: New ways of viewing access. S. Kroeger & J. Schuck (Eds.), *Responding to disability issues in student affairs*. (pp. 5-16) 64, San Francisco, CA: Jossey-Bass.

Johnson, D. (September 22, 1995). More scorn and less money dim law's lure. (pp. A1, A24).

Jordan, C. (1995, September). *Learning disabilities at the graduate or professional school level: Identification, acceptance and accommodation*. Paper presented at Higher Education and Students with Learning Disabilities: Learning in Learning Conference, sponsored by Curry College, Milton, MA.

Kincaid, J. M. (1992, July). *Compliance requirements of the ADA and Section 504*. Paper presented at the Association on Higher Education and Disability conference, Long Beach, CA.

Kincaid, J.M. (1995, June). *Legal aspects of accommmodating students with learning disabilities*. Postsecondary Learning Disability Training Institute, University of Connecticut, Farmington, CT.

Lerner, J. W., Lowenthal, B., & Lerner, S. R. (1995). *Attention deficit disorders-Assessment and teaching*. Pacific Grove, CA: Brooks/Cole Publishing.

National Joint Committee on Learning Disabilities. (1994). *Collective perspectives on issues affecting learning disabilities*. Austin, TX: PRO-ED.

Rothstein, L. F. (1990). *Special education and the law*. new York: Longman.

Scott, S. (1990). Coming to terms with the "otherwise qualified" student with a learning disability. *Journal of Learning Disabilities, 23*, 398-405.

Shapiro, J. (1996). Facing a painful dilemma. *America's Best Colleges*, U.S News & World Report. 37-39.

Shaywitz, S. E. & Shaw, R. (1988). The admissions process: An approach to selecting learning disabled students at the most selective colleges. *Learning Disabilities Focus, 3* (2), 81-86.

Tomlan, P., Farrell, M., & Geis, J. (1990). The 3's of staff development: Scope, sequence and structure. In J. J. Vander Putten (Ed.), *Proceedings of the 1989 AHSSPPE Conference* (pp. 23-32). Columbus, OH. AHSSPPE.

U.S. News & World Report (1995). Is Grad School Worth It? *America's Best Graduate Schools*, p. 8-11.

University of California at Berkeley (1995). *Model for accomodation: the academic needs of students with disabilities.* Berkeley, CA: Author.

University of Tennessee-Memphis (1995). *Technical standards for medical school admission and graduation.* College of Medicine. Memphis:TN.

Vogel, S. A. (1993). A retrospective and prospective view of post-secondary education for adults with learning disabilities. In S. A. Vogel & P. B. Adelman (Eds.), *Success for college students with learning disabilities*, (pp. 3-20). New York: Springer-Verlag.

Payne

Carnevale, A. P., Gainer, L. J., & Meltzer, A. S. (1988). *Workplace basics: The skills employers want.* Summary of research conducted under a two-year joint project of the American Society for Training and Development and the U.S. Department of Labor; Alexandria, Virginia.

Crawford, R. (Summer, 1995). *Developing strategic social skills.* LINKAGES, 2, 2, 9-10.

Dent, H. S., Jr. (1995). *Job Shock: Four new principles transforming our work and business.* New York: St. Martin's Press.

The Emily Hall Tremaine Foundation. (1995, March). *Learning disabilities and the American public: A look at America's awareness and knowledge.*

Equal Employment Opportunity Commission and the U.S. Department of Justice (1991). *Americans with disabilities act handbook.* Washington, D.C.: U.S. Government Printing Office.

Gerber, P. J., Ginsberg, R. J., & Reiff, H. B. (1992, October). Identifying alterable patterns in employment success for highly successful adults with learning disabilities. *Journal of Learning Disabilities, 25,* 8, 475-487.

Gingrich, N. (1995). *To renew America.* New York: Harper Collins.

Hallett, J. J. (1987). *Worklife visions: Redefining work for the informa-*

tion economy. Alexandria, Virginia: American Society for Personnel Administration.

Hammer, M. & Champy, J. (1993). *Reengineering the corporation.* New York: Harper Collins.

Koch, R. J. (1994). *Essential metacognitive skills in the workplace: A study of the fast food and retail industries.* Research paper presented to the faculty of Pacific Lutheran University: Tacoma, Washington.

Learning Disabilities Association of America. (1996) *They speak for themselves: A survey of adults with learning disabilities.* Pittsburgh, Pennsylvania: Shoestring Press.

McLaughlin, P. J., Loehr, J. E., & Simons, R. (1994). *Mentally Tough.* Pacific Mountain Enterprise and Peter J. McLaughlin.

National Alliance of Business. (1986). *Employment policies: Looking to the year 2000.* Washington, D.C.

National Center on Education and the Economy. (1990). *America's choice: High skills or low wages!.* The report of the Commission on the Skills of the American Workforce.

Office of Financial Management. (1991, January 18). *Investing in workforce excellence.* A summary of findings form the Investment in Human Capital Study.

Schaeffer, E. F. (March 1988). *Employment policies: looking to the year 2000.* In Workforce New and 2000 Match or Mismatch? Summary report of the Washington State Institute for Public Policy Conference, Olympia, Washington, January 15, 1988.

State of Washington. (1994). *High skills, high wages: Washington's comprehensive plan for workforce training and education.* Olympia, Washington: Author, (p. 19).

Unger, P. (1995). Culture shock: Tips for transitioners. *Management Review, 84,* 6, p.44.

University of Washington Northwest Policy Center (1996). *The changing northwest, 8,* 1.

U.S. Department of Labor (1993). The American workforce: 1992-2005. *Occupational Outlook Quarterly, 37,* 3, 2-3.

Gregg

Ackerman, P. L., Kyllomen, P. C., & Roberts, R. D. (1999) *Learning and individual differences: Process, trait, and content determinants.* Washington, D.C.: American Psychological Association.

Argyle, M. (Ed). (1969). *Social interaction.* Chicago: Aldine-

Atherton.

Argyle, M., & Cook, M. (1976). *Gaze and mutual gaze*. Cambridge: Cambridge University Press.

Birdwhistle, R.L. (1952). *Introduction to kinesics*. Louisville: University of Louisville Press.

Blalock, J. (1987). Auditory language disorders. In D. J. Johnson & J. W. Blalock (Eds.), *Adults with learning disabilities* (pp. 81-105). Orlando, Florida: Grune & Stratton.

Bruck, M. (1992). Persistence of dyslexics' phonological awareness deficits. *Developmental Psychology, 28* (5), 874-886.

Chafe, W. & Danielewicz, J. (1987). Properties of spoken and written language. In R. Horowitz & S. J. Samuels (Eds.), *Comprehending oral and written language* (pp. 83-113). San Diego, CA: Academic Press, Inc.

Cooper, A. (1988). Given-new: Enhancing coherence through cohesiveness. *Written Communication, 5* (3), 27-35.

Cox, B. E., Shanahan, T., & Sulzby, E. (1990). Good and Poor Elementary Readers' Use of Cohesion in Writing. *Reading Research Quarterly, 25*(1), 47-65.

Englert, C.S. (1992). Writing instruction from a sociocultural perspective: The holistic, dialogic, and social enterprise of writing. *Journal of Learning Disabilities, 25* (3), 153-172.

Englert, C. S. & Mariage, T. V. (1991). Sharing understandings: Structuring the writing experience through dialogue. *Journal of Learning Disabilities, 24* (6), 330-342.

Faigel, H. C., Doak, E., Howard, S. D., & Sigel, M. L. (1992). Emotional disorders in learning disabled adolescents. *Child Psychiatry and Human Development, 23,*1, 31-40.

Fuster, J.M (1995). Memory and planning: Two temporal perspectives of frontal lobe function. In H. H. Jasper, S. Riggio & P. S. Goldman-Rakic (Eds.), *Epilepsy and the functional anatomy of the frontal lobe* (pp. 9-18). New York: Raven Press.

Gregg, N. (1985). College learning disabled, normal, and basic writers: A comparison of frequency and accuracy of cohesive ties. *Journal of Psychoeducational Assessment, 3*, 223-231.

Gregg, N. & Jackson, R. (1989). Dialogue patterns of the nonverbal learning disabilities population-mirrors of self-regulation deficits. *Learning Disabilities: A Multidisciplinary Journal, 1*, 63-71.

Halliday, M.A.K. (1987). Spoken and written modes of meaning. In R. Horowitz & S. J. Samuels (Eds.), *Comprehending oral and written lan-*

guage (pp. 55-82). San Diego, CA: Academic Press, Inc.

Harnishfeger, K.K. & Bjorklund, D. F. (1994). A developmental perspective on individual differences in inhibition. *Learning and Individual Differences, 6, 3*, 331-355.

Harper, R., Wren, A., & Matarzzo, J. (eds.) (1978). *Nonverbal communication: The state of the art.* New York: John Wiley.

Horowitz, R. & Samuels, S. J. (1987). Comprehending oral and written language: Critical contrasts for literacy and schooling. In R. Horowitz & S. J. Samuels (Eds.), *Comprehending oral and written language* (pp. 1-52). San Diego, CA: Academic Press, Inc.

Hoy, C. & Gregg, N. (1994). *Assessment: The special educator's role.* Pacific Grove, California: Brooks/Cole Publishing Company.

Jackson, R. (1988). *Adults with nonverbal learning disabilities and their roles in achieving independence: A qualitative study.* Unpublished dissertation, University of Georgia.

Johnson, D. (1987). Disorders of written language. In D. J. Johnson & J. W. Blalock (Eds.), *Adults with learning disabilities: Clinical studies.* Orlando, FL: Grune and Stratton.

Johnson, D. (1987). Disorders of nonverbal learning disabilities. In D. J. Johnson & J. W. Blalock (Eds.), *Adults with learning disabilities: Clinical studies.* Orlando, FL: Grune and Stratton.

Johnson, D. & Myklebust, H.R. (1967). *Learning disabilities: Educational principles and practices.* New York: Gruen & Stratton.

Kintsch, W. & van Dijk, T. (1978). Toward a model of text comprehension and production. *Psychological Review, 85,* 363-394.

Klein, H. B., Moses, N., & Altman, E. (1988). Communication of adults with learning disabilities: Self and others' perceptions. *Journal of Communication Disorders, 21,*423-436.

Landa, R., Folstein, S. E. & Isaacs, C. (1991). Spontaneous narrative-discourse performance of parents of autistic individuals. *Journal of Speech and Hearing Research, 34,* 1339-1345.

Litowitz, B. (1987). Problems of conceptualization and language: Evidence from definitions. In D. J. Johnson & J. W. Blalock (Eds.) *Adults with learning disabilities* (pp. 131-143). Orlando, FL: Grune & Stratton.

Lyon, J. (1975). Deixis as the source of reference. In E.L. Keenan (ed.), *Formal semantics of natural language.* Cambridge, England: Cambridge University Press.

Morris, M. & Leuenberger, J. (1990). A report of cognitive, academic and linguistic profiles for college students with and without learning disabilities. *Journal of Learning Disabilities,23,*355-360.

Myklebust, H. (1975). Nonverbal learning disabilities. In H.R. Myklebust (Ed.), *Progress in learning disabilities: Vol.3.* (pp. 85-121).

Nystrand, M. (1987). The role of context in written communication. In R. Horowitz & S. J. Samuels (Eds.), *Comprehending oral and written language* (pp. 197-214). San Diego, CA: Academic Press, Inc.

Podhajski, B. (1998). Reading through sounds. *Linkages, 5,*1, pp. 1-4.

Raskind, M. H., Higgins, E. L., Goldberg, R. J. & Herman, K. L. (1998). Patterns of change and predictors of success in individuals with learning disabilities: Results from a twenty-year longitudinal study. *Thalamus, 16,*2, 40-64.

Rees, N. (speaker) (1988). *Pragmatics: A retrospective analysis.* (cassette recording H 8118-110). Rockville, MD: American Speech Language Hearing Association.

Rieber, R. W. & Carton, A. S. (Eds.) (1987-1997). *The collected works of L. S. Vygotsky* (Vols. 1 & 4). New York, NY: Plenum Press.

Rock, E. E., Fessler, M. A., & Church, R. P. (1997). The concomitance of learning disabilities and emotional/behavioral disorders: A conceptual model. *Journal of Learning disabilities,30,*3, 245-263.

Roth, F. & Spekman, N. J. (1994). Oral story production in adults with learning disabilities. In R. L. Bloom, L. K. Obler, S. DeCanti, & J. S. Ehrlich (Eds.), *Discourse analysis and applications: Studies in adult clinical populations* (pp. 131-147). Hillsdale, NJ: Lawrence Erlbaum Associates, Publishers.

Rourke, B. P., (1995). *Syndrome of NLD: Neurodevelopment manifestations.* New York: Guilford Press.

Rourke, B. P., Young, G. C., Strang, J. D. & Russell, D. L. (1986). Outcomes of childhood central processing deficiencies. In L.Grant & K.M. Adams (Ed.), *Neuropsychological assessment of neuropsychiatric disorders* (pp. 244-267). New York: Oxford University Press.

Stone, A. C. (1987). Abstract reasoning and problem solving. In D. J. Johnson & J. W. Blalock (Eds.), *Adults with learning disabilities* (pp. 131-143). Orlando, FL: Grune & Stratton.

Strang, J. D. & Rourke, B. P. (1985). Adaptive behavior of children who exhibit specific arithmetic disabilities and associated neuropsychological abilities and deficits. In B.P. Rourke (Ed.), *Neuropsychology of learning disabilities: Essentials of subgroup analysis* (pp. 302-328). New York: Guilford Press.

Vygotsky, L. S. (1962). *Thought and language*, E. Hanfmann & G. Vakar (trans.). Cambridge, MA: The M.I.T. Press. (Original work published 1934).

Wallach, G. & Liebergott, J. W. (1984). Who shall be called "learning disabled"? Some new directions. In G. Wallach & K. Butler (Eds.), *Language learning disabilities in school-age children* (pp. 1-14). Baltimore: Williams and Wilkins.

White,W. J. (1992). The postschool adjustment of persons with learning disabilities: Current status and future projections. *Journal of Learning Disabilities, 25,7,* 448-274.

Wiig, E. H. (1996). Language and communication disorders in adults with learning disabilities. In N. Gregg, C. Hoy & A. Gay (Eds.), *Adults with learning disabilities: Theoretical and practical perspectives* (pp. 232-260). New York: Guilford Press.

Wiig, E. H. & Secord, W.A. (1991). *Measurement and assessment: A marriage worth saving.* Chicago: Riverside.

Wiig, E. H. & Secord, W.A. (1992). *Test of Word Knowledge.* San Antonio, TX: Psychological Corporation.

Books Edited by Teresa Allissa Citro

The Experts Speak: Parenting the Child with Learning Disabilities
(This book is also available in Spanish.)

"This distinguished group of authors presents a brilliant collection of articles. The multidisiplinary viewpoints, perspectives and strategies focus on academic, collaborative, social, psychological and family issues. *The Experts Speak* is an excellent resource for professionals, parents and everyone facing the daily challenges of learning and attentional differences."

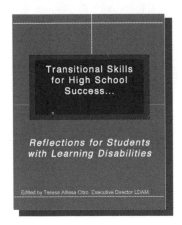

Transitional Skills for High School Success...Reflections for Students with Learning disabilities

"The road to postsecondary education is not well-paved and it contains detours, roadblocks and pot-holes that students and parents must consider. This latest LDAM publication provides them with a road map and some sage advice from individuals who have traveled that road. The articles, essays and chapters provide pragmatic and useful information– and a dose of inspiration, as well."

Videos Produced by Teresa Allissa Citro
These videos are only available in English.

Einstein and Me: Talking about Learning Disabilities

Kids speak openly and honestly about:
•How they found out about their learning disability.
•The policies and people who made life difficult.
•People and programs that helped them cope.
•Their strengths and talents.
•Their futures.

Meeting with Success: Tips for a Successful IEP

It's easy to find dozens of documents explaining the IEP process, but an IEP meeting can turn into an adversarial nightmare even if everybody involved understands the "rules and regulations." **It doesn't have to be this way!** In this upbeat and optimistic video, narrated by Dr. Jerome Schultz, you'll observe "real" parents, teachers, administrators and other specialists as they demonstrate *Tips for Meeting with Success.*

Stop and Go Ahead with Success; As integrated approach to helping children develop social skills.

Friendships are critical for our sense of well being. This video offer practical solutions for teachers and parents on how to address the social problems children with learning disabilities in elementary school face. It demonstrates an integrated approach to teaching social skills as they arise throughout the school day. When parents, teachers and other adults work together to coach children on these skills, childrens become more confident and enter social situations anticipating SUCCESS.

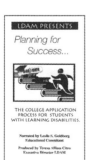

Planning for Success: The College Application Process for Students with Learning Disabilites

In this video you will observe the college application process for one student with a learning disability.
Individuals vary in strenghts and weaknesses and yet all students have the ability to reach their full potential when carefully planning for success.

Videos Produced by Teresa Allissa Citro
These videos are only available in English.

Pathways to Success: College Students with Learning Disabilities

Students with learning disabilities share the strategies that have brought them success both at the graduate and undergraduate levels. They discuss the realities of adjusting to the new academic challenges and to the differences in support services between postsecondary and high school levels.

Profiles of Success: Successful Adults Achieving with Learning Disabilities

Larry B. Silver interviews young adults with learning disabilities about their experiences. In this video, meet three exceptional adults with learning disabilities who achieved success. Hear how they struggled and overcame obstacles and chose careers that best used their strengths. Let their stories of hope, fortitude and resilience encourage you. Dr. Silver goes on to explain what learning disabilities are and how teachers and parents can help every student with learning disabilities become "Profiles of Success."

Portraits of Success: Fostering Hope and Resilience in Individuals with Learning Disabilities

This video features interviews by Larry B. Silver, M.D. and Robert Brooks, Ph.D. with adults, parents and teachers about their experiences with learning disabilities. These "Portraits of Success" will foster hope and resilience in children with learning disabilities.

To order books or Videos
Please visit our website at www.LDAM.org
or call LDAM at 781-891-5009

Join LDAM Today!

LDAM is a non-profit, volunteer organization. Its financial support comes from membership dues, conference proceeds, grants and donations. LDAM policies are determined by elected officers and a Board of Directors. Your contributions are greatly needed. **Contributions to LDAM are tax deductible.**

Membership Includes

- Annual membership in Learning Disabilities Association of America and Learning Disabilities Association of Massachusetts
- Six LDA newsbrief publications.
- Tri-Annual issues of "The Journal of the Learning Disabilities Association of Massachusetts."
- Notification of conferences
- Reduced registration fees at conferences and workshops (including the International LDA Conference, Massachusetts regional LDA conferences, and the Joint Conference on Learning Disabilities)
- Information about resources and services pertaining to learning disabilities, "Yearly Directory on Learning Disabilities."
- New member packet information

Membership Information

Name _____   Date _____

Address _____   ❏ Professional

City _____   ❏ Institutional

State/Zip _____   ❏ Student

Telephone _____   ❏ Adult

Interests

I am willing to work on the following committees:

___ Public Relations ___ Fund Raising
___ Multi Cultural ___ Conferences
___ Grants ___ Legislative
___ Development ___ Speakers Bureau
___ Research and Dissemination
___ Educational (K-Post Secondary

Please enroll me as a member of the Learning Disabilities Association of Massachusetts: ___ New ___ Renew

___ Individual (Family) $40.00
___ Professional $60.00
___ Foreign $65.00
___ Institutional $100
___ Tax Deductible Contribution _____

Institutional members receive a 10% discount to exhibit at our conferences, a 10% discount for ads placed in the Gazette and pre-conference brochures, and unlimited attendance at member's fee to the conferences.

Make checks payable to **LDAM.**
Send to **LDAM, P.O. Box 142, Weston, MA 02493** or
Register online at **www.LDAM.org**